Journey to Cassadaga

Journey to Cassadaga

My Spiritual Awakening

Jeanette Strack-Zanghi

Writers Club Press

San Jose New York Lincoln Shanghai

Journey to Cassadaga
My Spiritual Awakening

Writers Club Press
an imprint of iUniverse, Inc.

For information address:
iUniverse, Inc.
5220 S. 16th St., Suite 200
Lincoln, NE 68512
www.iuniverse.com

ISBN: 0-595-22013-4

Printed in the United States of America

There is only one person this book could be dedicated to—the person who helped conceive the idea of the book; the person who is part of the journey; Spiritualist, Medium, and Healer, to a God-like kind of man......Donald J. Zanghi.

Contents

Preface

The book will tell you of my journey, how I found the Spiritualist Camp, what I learned of the Truth of God, what I learned of my past lives, and how I was led to Cassadaga to be reunited with my soul mate. The purpose of this book is to demystify Spiritualism.

The story is factual, however persons are given fictitious names.

1

The Journey: I discover Colby Temple

This is not fiction, but many of the events will sound like fiction. This is not about witchcraft in a Southern Spiritualist Temple but there are two supernatural events. This is the true story of my journey to Cassadaga: the story of finding my God and my soul-mate. As surely as the tide is pulled by the moon, so I was unwittingly drawn to the town of Cassadaga.

My status was boredom. I had retired from teaching and insurance sales. It seemed that all my life I had searched for something, but what? I began to wonder what purpose I was serving.

I had been taking Mom to a fundamentalist Christian Church each Sunday. I loved the group singing, but was unimpressed with the remaining ritual. My younger friend, Maggie (four doors west) and I had discussed Cassadaga. She had attended a spiritualist church in Michigan. So one Sunday I made an excuse to Mom and began the journey of a lifetime. Later, I learned it was not an accidental journey: there are no accidents. It was created of my own design, out of my search for God.

"This should be an adventure," Maggie said as I hooked up the seat belt. Mag is 4Oish, and suffers from psoriasis. We were neighbors, and on quite friendly terms.

"Well, I wouldn't want Mom to know where I'm going. She'd be sure I was cavorting with witches if I mentioned mediums and healers.

Good grief, I think I heard the mediums even believe they can talk to the dead!"

"I wonder where Christ fits into their philosophy," Maggie pondered. We were now out of town and heading West towards Deland. The road was flat, slightly curving and bordered on each side by typical Florida "bush": palmetto, coarse grass and scraggly pine. I always thought the pine deplorable compared to the tall magnificent pine of the Adirondack Mountains of New York from where I hail.

"Buffy was up to her usual tricks this morning," she laughed. We were both cat lovers. She has one cat to my five furry friends. "She was pushing books off the shelves again." We both laugh because Mag collects books: she <u>collects</u> books, she rarely <u>reads</u> them. I just howled when she told me. "But why would you just collect them?" I queried. "I don't know. But when I see a bunch of books I just have to buy them."

"Maybe, the mediums can tell you," I said with a wicked grin.

My mind took one of it's giant leaps and I was celebrating my birthday, my birthday of a month prior. I remember raising the champagne glass to my lips and laughing with my younger lover. To him, I was still blonde and attractive. But I was tired of everything. It seemed when I had retired from my varied careers (boutique owner, newspaper columnist, English teacher, insurance agent); I had retired from <u>LIFE</u>. I was tired of being the material girl: buying, buying, buying—things to replace the emptiness.

What a maze. The road twisted this way and that like following a treasure map. Would I really find a treasure—that thought intrigued me. Then hills, what were hills doing in this area? We passed small bungalows, a large brick house, and a fence-enclosed estate. Finally, the sign Cassadaga.

"Wow, we're really here. And early. Shall we ride around the town first?" Mag asked.

"Yes, I already feel an energy here, don't you?"

"You're right, like we really aren't in Florida—like another place and time—a different force field." We passed a huge two-story hotel, antiquated. "Let's try Stevens." Mag said. We passed another big building, of weathered wood, sloping roofs, and sporting an old-fashioned front porch: the Andrew Jackson Davis building. It also housed a book store.

"Bet it's full of new age stuff," I commented. Little did I know it sold some of the Eckankar books I had already been reading. We passed an unpainted two—story building—Harmony Hall. Was it residential? These structures must be one hundred years old. And on past Colby Temple, past Spirit Pond-(that name gave me shivers). Wonder how you would feel here at night!

"Here we go," Mag said as we headed up a rather steep hill on Lake St. I found myself riding past weathered wooden houses that could have been straight out of a New England coastal town. One sign said Winter Heaven House (white with pink trim). A charming tan and brown house belonged to the Reverends Nick and Jean Sourant. We rode past the white with blue trimmed Patty Aubrey house, the Louis Gates house, that would play a part in my Future, then right on Seneca and back to Colby Temple.

"We didn't see much of the town, but enough to know it's different than other parts of Florida." Mag commented.

We were still early as we stood in front of Colby Memorial Temple. It certainly didn't look like anything I thought of as a temple: I visualized a temple from India: shiny, bright, ornate. No, this was a solid rectangular building of stucco and brick reminiscent of a big, tan school house. Six long windows with carved arches graced the front. The only concession to trim was a carved facade at the top of the structure. The temple seemed rooted in the ground, solid, indomitable. Directly to our right was a small, octagonal-shaped building. Caesar Forman Healing Center, we read, with Sunday healings from '10 to 10:30. "Shall we?" I ventured.

Mag looked skeptical. "The door is closed, shall we peek in?" Mag still hung back—Mag who is usually the more aggressive one. Walking to the door, I was uncertain too, but I opened it and closed it abruptly. A man sat in a chair with his eyes closed while the healer extended hands over him. "Think I did the wrong thing," I exclaimed.

A moment later, the man exited and we entered, "I'm so sorry for interrupting," I told the pleasant looking healer, Jane Hall.

"Oh you could have walked right in and waited in one of the chairs," she said pointing to them. Mag sat on the stool for a healing. I picked up a booklet entitled 1995-1996 Annual Program of Cassadaga Spiritualist Camp. I sneaked a peek at Mag, her eyes closed while the healer had hands extended over her. Then I opened the book and found the following definitions:

SPIRITUALISM is the Science, Philosophy and Religion of continuous life, based upon the demonstrated fact of communication, by means of mediumship, with those who live in the Spirit World (1920)." Ah, so they did believe they could contact the dead!

SPIRITUALIST is one who believes, as the basis of his or her religion, in the Communication between this and the spirit world by means of mediumship, and who endeavors to mold his or her character and conduct in accordance with the highest teachings derived from such communion (1920)." Well, at least they are striving for the highest in character.

"MEDIUM is one whose organism is sensitive to vibrations from the spirit world and through whose instrumentality intelligences in that world are able to convey messages and produce the phenomena of Spiritualism (1929)." Oh, can't wait to meet one of these babies!

HEALER is one who either through his own inherent powers or through his mediumship, is able to impart vital, curative force to pathological conditions. (1930)."

I looked at Maggie as the healer was moving around her body, hands hovering. Then the hands were on her face, throat, back. She whispered something to her, and I knew I was up for grabs. I rolled my eyes at Mag and sat on the stool. The healer was near a receptacle behind me moving her hands: cleansing? I closed my eyes trying to make myself ready for the healing.

I had also just read in the book:

HEALING: 1. is an important and well-recognized aspect of the religion of Spiritualism, 2. is a natural step with God. Some healing's are instant, others take time and a change in life style. 3. Both healings and the laying on of hands are recorded in history, both old and new. 4. Healing can bring you the serenity and peace that is so essential to the well being of each of us. 5. Healing benefits body, mind and spirit."

As the healer approached me, I thought if it doesn't help my body maybe my <u>spirit</u> will be uplifted. I thought of God and willed myself quiet. I felt her presence behind me, her hands over me, and finally her hands touching my neck. When she touched my back her hands <u>trembled</u>. I could feel her trembling, but nothing else. She finally told me to go with God and we left the Healing Center.

"Did you feel that trembling?" I asked Mag.

"Yes, when she touched my back her hands trembled with <u>energy</u>. But I really didn't <u>feel</u> differently did you?"

"No, but I just read in this booklet that some healings take time to work." We walked to the temple; people outside greeted us. Inside, we were handed hymnals and the August church schedule. We noticed a book, a book where you could list people for absent healing by mediums and ministers with the daily meditations. I could think of a page full who needed prayer including myself. You could even list pets. So I listed my sick Siamese, CC, and my daughter-in-law, who had on a mere whim decided not to speak to me, and Mom who is narrow in viewpoint and finally myself in all my judgmental glory.

We found a long bench in the back, there were also regular pews. There were actually three areas of seating. The floor pitched forward like a floor in an old Broadway theatre. Mag and I took rear seats, trying to be inconspicuous. It was a simply decorated church, almost stark. The curved arch windows allowed ample sunlight. The eye was drawn to the podium area. An organ and several chairs a lectern. The bounding area was trimmed with a purple flounce. Sunflowers (pictorial) appeared to be their flower. Side wall pictures were of Indian men and women (and wouldn't mother faint) in juxtaposition a picture of Jesus and Buddha.

Mag looked around, and I pondered the religious ideas I had brought with me to Cassadaga. From my childhood, from my Catholic Christianity, I had learned that God was three persons in one: Father, Son and Holy Ghost. Jesus was willingly sacrificed on a cross to save us from our sins. He took on our sins to give us salvation and eternal life. BUT we must follow the ten commandments and the ways of Christ or we would be lost—go to purgatory for punishment or to the burning lake of fire. In middle age I began to question my Catholic—and later, Presbyterian teachings.

If God loved us unconditionally—even more than we humans loved our children-how could he put us in a lake of burning fire? If my child murdered someone or was dangerous to society, I could restrict him from society, I could try every conceivable means to rehabilitate him. But could I place him in eternal fire? NO, NO, NO. The God who is so far above ~ human love could not do this either, I thought. ·

My mind still flitted after my beliefs as the church began to fill, and the organist began a peculiar kind of melody. The Bible says God is a jealous God. Jealousy is really a combination of fear and anger,…very negative emotions. Do I believe God (who is love) could have those emotions. NO, NO, NO. Jesus gave up his life for us to compensate for "our" sins. Therefore if we sin and are truly sorry, our sins are wiped away. There seems to be an imbalance here between the mini sinner and the maxi sinner. The liar and the murderer get the same treatment. What's so fair about that?

A few years ago a friend handed me some books about Eckankar, the ancient religion of soul travel. Some precepts that came as shocks of recognition were: we are all sparks of God and he wants all his sparks returned to him. Yes, we will all return to God. I had always toyed with the idea of reincarnation. We will be born and reborn until we are perfected. There are natural laws of cause and effect. We are all responsible for our own actions. We will eventually learn become aware, return to God. There are many levels of heaven (Biblical: "in my father's house there are many mansions"). These were the beliefs I brought with me on this journey to Cassadaga.

"Do you like the music?" Mag whispered.

"A little strange," I replied. Four people walked to the podium; the church rustle stilled. I wondered if the service would be like the fundamentalist Christian service I had attended last week with Mom. There had been a session of singing, a list of announcements, the pleading for money-(you don't prosper if you don't tithe), the sermon that reiterated you were a SINNER, and if unrepentant were plunged into an eternal "lake of burning fire." It concluded with a long "alter call" meant to intimidate you into coming forward (with every eye on you) to openly admit being a sinner and to receive absolution when you openly confessed Christ as your savior. This is what I was accustomed to, but I found something quite startlingly different. A chairperson walked to the lectern. She directed a child to light the candles that represented body, mind and spirit of Spirituality. Light streamed in from the eight side windows. My eye caught a glimpse of another photo: Mother Theresa. My eyes rested on the potted trees in the front corners, then back to the lectern. The chairperson explained the service would be in three parts: the healing portion, the lecture and the message service. I punched Mag, "You want a message, don't you." Her eyes glowed in affirmation. Me? I just preferred to remain inconspicuous and observe. My friends would laugh at that—I usually wear very outstanding hats—so what's with the inconspicuous.

The healing portion began. I looked back as people flocked to the side benches. There were several colorful stools lined up across the entire back of the church. Some people walked to the stools while those on the benches waited their turns.

Donald Zanghi, student medium, walked to the lectern to lead the healing meditation. We read in unison the healing prayer. Those of us remaining in our seats, could follow the guided meditation healing. We were asked to remove papers or books from our laps, to place our feet on the floor, close our eyes.

Soothing music accompanied the meditation. We were asked to image angels around us. The angels were going to take us on a journey. We were taken up, up, to a beautiful crystal palace. I felt wonderful as I imagined myself accompanied by angels in front of a palace of crystal. "This palace can be any color you want," Donald Zanghi told us. My palace was all sparkling clear crystal. Then we were told to enter the palace where there was a room with a beautiful comfortable chair. There would be healing guides coming to us for healing of body, mind and spirit. Several guides came forth for the body including Hippocrates. I chose him, and felt the healing force he offered me. I was really getting into this imaginary trip. I began to feel very tranquil. Then we were introduced to healers for the mind, and I chose Jung. I allowed the healing vibes to soothe me. And finally we were offered healers for the spirit, and I chose Jesus. I asked for the healing power of Jesus. Then we were told the angels were coming for us, and they took us out the door and homeward. We were asked to mentally shrink the palace—(the healing palace) and place it in our hearts. "You are the temple: the temple is within you," Donald Zanghi concluded. The others had now returned to their seats. We were to sing a song of praise. I stood, wobbled. The song began and Mag looked at me as my words didn't come. I was still in the tranquil state of the meditation and didn't want to be disturbed.

The principles of Spiritualists were read in unison: Mag held the book and we began to read. I was determined to read only what I presently believed. 1. "We believe in Infinite Intelligence." I could go with that: God surely is that. 2. "We believe that the phenomena of nature, both physical and spiritual, are the expression of Infinite Intelligence." Again, yes, the physical and the spiritual all reflect God. 3. "We affirm that a correct understanding of such expression and living in accordance therewith constitute true religion"…ring those bells! Right on! You must live your religion daily. 4. "We affirm that the existence and personal identity of the individual continue after the change called death." Yes, yes, yes and amen. I glanced at the next principle and stopped reading. I just wasn't too sure I believed this one. 5. "We affirm that communication with the so-called dead is a fact, scientifically proven by the phenomena of Spiritualism." That all remained in the "maybe, prove it to me stage." 6. "We believe that the highest morality is contained in the Golden Rule: "What-so-ever ye would that others should do unto you, do ye also unto them." What a wonderful world if we all practiced that one. 7. "We affirm the moral responsibility of the individual, and that he makes his own happiness or unhappiness as he obeys or disobeys Nature's physical and spiritual laws." That sort of kicks "fate" in the fanny, and says you have the responsibility for you. O.K. 8. "We affirm that the doorway to reformation is never closed against any human soul here or hereafter." That's where I differ from Mom who thinks of eternal damnation. I always thought the door was eternally open. AGREED. 9. "We affirm that the precepts of Prophecy and Healing contained in the Bible are Divine attributes proven through Mediumship." They are divine attributes, but I would have to <u>observe</u> if they were proven by Mediumship. For principles of a new religion (to me) I'd say I believe in ninety percent already, I thought.

The chairperson now read the various announcements, and the collection plate was passed. <u>No</u> begging for extra funds, just blessing the giver.

"Here we go with the "sock-it-to us you sinner" lecture I whispered to Mag as the Rev. Wayne Hobson began his message. But, I had a pleasant surprise in store. He reflected about how much time do people really spend exploring their potential. Look at the best and the worst and decide if we can do something <u>to change</u>. Realize we carry Divinity in us—as parts of God we carry <u>unlimited potential</u>. We are individual, like grains of sand, and we each have our pathway to God. But, how can we find the pathway? Be aware of the <u>decisions</u> you make. Are they motivated by <u>FEAR</u>? The journey is important. We create opportunities. "Mistakes" cause you to grow—in reality there are no mistakes. But we must beware of fear (and recognize it), and guilt (a real block). Love is the greatest concept. Love yourself. We never give ourselves an even break. We even block compliments. You must respect yourself as a talented, divine being. Inside you is God, all you need for happiness is there. Money won't make you happy. Abundance is there for you: how you love and how others love you. <u>Patience</u> gives you time to bear witness as things unfold. We must have patience for the world to be perfected, desires fulfilled, to unlock the door to self. God knows how beautiful you are and is waiting for <u>you</u> to know it. Your higher self knows it. Your <u>outer</u> self <u>sees</u> it but doesn't <u>know</u> it. This is a cycle-we will be in spirit-we will be back. Be kind to yourself. God is in us."

"I don't believe it," I whispered to Maggie. "He actually told us we had potential—that we were really part of God—or God-like." I felt wonderful: my heart swelled. I was basically good—not evil—not a horrible sinner to be condemned. What a difference an uplifting lecture can make. I felt powerful and ready to embrace my fellow-man. Wow, I felt <u>GOOD</u>.

There were more songs and then the final part of the service: the messages. The medium Ben Thomas came forward and told us to look or be aware of what we were wearing because that is how he would identify us. I knew Maggie wanted to be read, as she glanced down at her purple tunic. But, alas the medium looked to the other aisle and identified "The man in the green shirt. I feel a disturbance. Be aware of the people around you. Reach out to the situation—don't have fear. I also get a vibration of a mother and grandmother. These entities had a bit of spiritualism, but not enough. They want your help (your prayers). We help each other on both sides. Also an envelop, long overdue, will be coming to you."

The Rev. Ben turned and wanted to talk to the man in a black shirt. "Your name? Bobby" (mediums often wanted to hear the voice of the person). "I sense you should go in a new direction. Go with faith that God will be with you. Listen to yourself. I see a gentleman from Spirit close to you—someone who had been in the military. His message is 'Why are you doing this to yourself. Do not listen to others. And to a lady named Sylvia, Ben told her he was aware of a child who passed about a year ago. The spirit stood behind her and related 'You called me by a special name.'"

The medium thanked us and returned to his seat. I was fascinated. Ben Thomas spoke of viewing people from the spirit world: grandfathers, friends, mothers that had passed on. Mediums (supposedly) were seeing them. Yes, they <u>described</u> these entities. And the medium actually gave the person a message from spirit. How the heck could they see things I couldn't see? Were they just imaging all this? Yet, from the description of the dead relatives, the person being read, could relate, "Yes, that is exactly what my grandmother was like?" The mediums looked into the future, gave advice, told you if you were on the right track. At this point I couldn't believe or disbelieve. But, I wanted to know more. I <u>had</u> to know more—to explore these concepts.

After another song and the final benediction, we trooped from the temple. We had been invited to the Andrew Jackson Davis Building for refreshments and to remain for more messages. The building was located a very short distance up the road, past the houses of mediums and past residential halls: old, wonderful weathered relics of the past. "Wonder what the refreshments are?" Mag pondered.

"Whatever, I'm suddenly ravenous," I replied. We walked through an entry hall and into a cavernous room set up with several rows of long tables, many long benches in the rear. To the left two long tables groaned under the weight of coffee urns and a sumptuous array of breakfast goodies. If you wanted to donate, there were donation jars. I had coffee and loaded a little plate with Danish and a bagel. "Not the tables," I warned, as I headed for the more inconspicuous benches lined against the back wall. I tried to balance food against coffee cup and realized the tables would be more accommodating.

I'd be darned if I'd sit there—might sit right beside one of those "mediums." What would I say to such a person? Would they be able to <u>read</u> all my <u>thoughts</u>? Boy, would I be in deep "do-do!" On the bench, Maggie sipped a drink, while I gobbled my goodies. All the benches were now filled, and people at the tables were deep in conversation and laughter.

At 12:30 a moderator welcomed us, led us in prayer, and introduced the first medium reader. I listened marveling at the spirits of relatives giving advice, at the advice on finances, affairs of the heart etc. "Your dying for a reading, right?" I whispered.

"Yes, maybe I could get a message about Grandma up there in Michigan, lying there vegetating from that stroke—or maybe some advice on whether I should stay on this job—or…"

"Stop, stop," I laughed, "you'd have them here until night just giving you messages." Another medium was introduced: The Rev. Ben Thomas. This was a very distinguished looking gentleman: dark suit—(well accessorized)—mustache. I was later to learn that he had had a long career as a school principal and had been a Spiritualist for over 20 years. He looked around and made a bee-line towards the benches—the benches where Mag and I sat. Oh, I knew, I knew it would be me, and I wanted to sink through the floor. But when he inquired if I wanted a reading I chickened out and said yes. It seemed every eye in the place was on me. But somehow, when he started talking his eyes held mine and I just heard his words. I know now he said many things to me but I mainly recall one thing. He said I was like the woman in the <u>Pilgrim</u> going from church to church on my quest or search, and that I went from person to person dispensing wisdom. Wow, not half bad I thought. Especially that dispensing of wisdom. But, at the moment I didn't feel very wise at all.

Outside, Maggie looked crestfallen. "I know you wanted a reading, and I just didn't care. But, I'm sure you'll get one the next time.

"We will return, won't we?" she asked.

And I knew—as <u>surely</u> <u>as</u> <u>the</u> <u>tide</u> is <u>pulled</u> by <u>the</u> <u>moon,</u> <u>I</u> <u>would</u> <u>return</u> <u>to</u> <u>Cassadaga</u>.

2

The first healing

I saw Peter (my lover) twice the following week. "How was the Spook trip?" He asked knowing I had gone to visit Colby Temple.

I was reluctant to discuss my trip. I knew he had been brought up in a fundamentalist Christian religion, and although non-practicing—the deep roots were still there. I'm sure he even felt some guilt about our love affair of many years. And so I answered, "The goblins didn't catch me, in fact I might even give them another chance."

Maggie came to visit one night and we looked at the Annual Program again and gleaned a few facts. "Hey look, Colby Temple is named after the founder: George Colby, born in 1848. And from my Empire state of New York (a town called Pike). He was a traveling (trance) medium and known as the 'Seer of Spiritualism'."

Mag peered over my shoulder. She had a fascination for angels. She said, "He had a <u>spirit</u> guide—an Indian named Seneca. <u>And</u> a German philosopher Wandah, who channeled the healings, <u>and</u> a Professor Huffman who worked on his public messages." Whee, I thought, this man couldn't miss when half the dead were working with him. And I began to wonder if I had someone working with me. If so, they were certainly falling down on the job—I didn't seem to be doing much that was creative. The last piece of work I had done was a <u>verse</u> written after I had taken care of a terminal ex-husband. I was there when he died, and a verse came to mind in time to be read at the funeral. When I thought of how <u>quickly</u> that verse popped into my mind—maybe, just maybe I <u>did</u> have help in creating.

Your Last Day

If I had known it was your last day,
I would not have washed your sheets,
And hung them out to dry.
If I had known it was your last day,
I would not have swept the floors,
Or cooked the evening meal.
Would not have wasted time on mundane chores,

If I had known it was your last day,
I would have held your hand in reminiscence,
Recalling 25 years in the Warrensburg house
Life with three special sons.

If I had known it was your last day,
We would have taken a vicarious journey,
Where you could have walked the sandy shores,
And basked in the Southern Sun.

But of a sudden, it was your last hour,
I held you close saying it was time to go,
That I would survive, that loved ones waited
On a distant shore
And on your last day, I kissed your soul good-bye.

It dawned on me with really clear knowledge, as I recalled the lines of that poem that yes, yes, I did have some kind of guidance with the writing. It came so fast, so <u>fast</u> that I could barely keep the pen in flow with the speed of my thoughts.

"And look, look," Mag exclaimed "it was the guide, Sencea who told George Colby in a message that he would be establishing a Spiritual community in the South. He got instructions that led him to Orange City and then through the wilds to an area George had seen in a seance—the area of Cassadaga. That was 1875." I could imagine the wilds of undergrowth in the area in that time period. George Colby must have felt like a true explorer.

"By 1895 the camp size was 57 acres and was incorporated. The first people came to nearby hotels until residences were erected—The style of cottages is quite unique for Florida housing," we learned. I certainly agreed with that, nothing of the Spanish style—more the look of New England cottages. The name "Camp" appears on the name, but there are no camping facilities. The book explains "Camp meeting" is actually an old term which was used to designate the annual gathering of religious groups. We learned many of the original buildings (library, auditorium, hotel, and pavilion) no longer stand today. But, the recreation hall—the Andrew Jackson Davis-building is in full use.

"Designated a Historic District on the National Register of Historic Places, the Southern Cassadaga Spiritualist Camp Meeting Association is the oldest active religious community in the Southeastern United States." I was totally impressed: this was actually a very well—known place throughout the country.

"Will you be going to the temple Sunday,? "Mag inquired.

"Nope it's the ritual: dinner with Mom Friday evening, and then on to <u>her</u> church on Sunday. But I'll let her know I'm busy the <u>following</u> Sunday." And so I went with Mom, and was totally aggravated by the long alter call.

"I think they expect us to go up," Mom whispered.

"Well, I already believe in Jesus, and I'll be darned if I'm going to go on public display just because they <u>expect</u> me to," I retorted.

In the meantime I added another doll to my collection of over fifty dolls. I had started the collection about two years ago. When people asked me why, I couldn't answer. Why was I so fascinated with these little faces? I just know I searched each face as if looking for something or someone.

The next Sunday I returned to Cassadaga. I had called my sister, Doris, and she accompanied us. She, too, had read my Eckankar books and was interested in a more spiritualistic religion. After the service she said, "Yes, yes, I'll be coming here as often as I can." We learned that there would be adult Sunday school classes prior to church (in September). It was for "those who have a desire to learn more about our Religion and Philosophy and may want to attend Adult Lyceum. A different teacher each week will provide an instructive format in which one may learn the truths of Spiritualism and other related subjects." Mag and I grinned in unison: we knew the Lyceum was for us. I felt excited just thinking of more personal contact with the mediums.

The end of August meant a return visit to upper New York State and to the little hamlet of Warrensburg, the hamlet nestled—cradled—in the splendid gold-red foliage of the mountains. I loved Florida and its beaches, but my heart always longed for my native mountains.

I stayed with my oldest son Winston who also had my youngest son, Nick and wife Suzanne, visiting. They were about to rent a house and reside in New York State after several years in Florida. We had a wonderful time shopping (my addiction to clothes and jewelry) and visiting my old friends. I also did mucho cooking for "the gang." I never mentioned my foray into Spiritualism to Nick and Suzanne. God forbid! They were born again, dyed in the wool, Fundamentalist Christians. They were expecting the immanent return of Christ and figured they would both be caught up in the "rapture." I guess they figured I would "luck" even if I was a sinner because Christ would so favor them that as the Mom I could fly along on Nick's coattails. Near the end of the trip, Nick and Suzanne had one of their infamous "misunderstandings." I trekked with her on an excursion to Lake George. I joined Nick for an early breakfast out. In all cases I let them do the complaining (about each other), while I tried to keep a judicious silence—only nodding my head at infrequent intervals. The day before I left, they were to see the marriage counselor. I was in the kitchen when she whizzed past me, and I sensed avoiding me. That night, after I had packed, Nick was in the kitchen and I asked him if Suzanne was upset with me for some unexplained reason.

"Oh, no, "he replied, "she will be out to say good-bye to you in a minute." The good-bye was icy, cold, and her embrace was that of a granite statue. For some reason she was blaming their misunderstanding on me.

I rode to the airport with Winston the next morning. I told him of Suzanne's sudden, cold treatment. "She's a born again Christian," I complained. "Aren't Christ's followers supposed to use compassion, understanding, and kindness in their dealings with other people? Even if she thought I had said or done something she didn't like, why couldn't she have discussed it with me instead of giving me this cold treatment?" And I remembered her in church mouthing the Scriptures along with the minister, running to her friends, her face wreathed in smiles. But in the real world, the world of husband and mother-in-law where was the religion? And I thought of the 6th principle of Spiritualism, "We believe the highest morality is contained in the Golden Rule: "Whatsoever ye would that others should do unto you, do ye also unto them."

Back in the hot, baking in the sun, Florida, I looked forward to my next trip to Cassadaga. Maggie had taken care of my five furry friends while I was gone. But, their loud meows of complaint let me know I had been missed. My kitties: my little furry friends. How akin in personality to people they were: Mark Anthony (Tony) black, tom-boy, with his jealous possessive disposition; Caesar (CC) the Siamese, the garrulous, talking companion; Puss-in-Boots (Bootsie) a tabby, the bully, who was king of the hill with the other cats and even had the audacity of trying to bully me; Tiger (Tiggie) a 20 pound hunk of golden fluff, the silent, loving one; and Bear-Bear (Rat, Brat), the diminutive black fuzzy (only) female, the smartest and most conniving of the pack—whose antics made me frantic. Yes, I thought, very akin to people.

One evening I reviewed some of my Cassadaga papers and discovered that the church schedule listed a September 14th candle light healing service. "This is a special healing service for those who need healing for the body, mind or spirit. Saturday evening in the Colby Temple, 7:30". I planned to be there: maybe I might even get some instantaneous results—although up to this point I hadn't seen that happen. Perhaps my healing required the waiting game. However, after my trip North, my Spirit sure could use a few <u>bandages.</u>

<u>And</u> <u>so</u> <u>began</u> <u>one</u> <u>of</u> <u>the</u> <u>major</u> <u>turning</u> <u>points</u> <u>in</u> <u>my</u> <u>religious</u> <u>belief</u> <u>s:</u> <u>The</u> <u>belief</u> <u>in</u> <u>Spiritualist</u> <u>healing</u>.

Maggie left work early and we made another "journey towards Cassadaga." We arrived early: thus we were among the first eight numbers. "Look," isn't it beautiful?" I said to Maggie. The church was illuminated by candles: beneath every window, surrounding the whole room. Candles, candles everywhere, flickering, casting an aura of peace, serenity, mystery. We sat transfixed in the twinkling glow. Subtle, unfamiliar music filled the room. The church filled, and there were prayers before the healings. Up front eight stools stood before the healers. Eight numbers were read. Mag had number six and I had number eight. She proceeded to a table where she was directed to light a candle place it in a holder, then retrieve it after the healing. She walked down the line stopping at the sixth stool. I followed, lit my candle, placed it in the holder, then proceeded towards the last seat in the row. I recognized my healer as Donald Zanghi (student medium). Students study for several years: I heard he was near the end of the study. I glanced at him, dapper in a tan suit. He sported a beard (perhaps to compensate for thinning hair.) I glanced into his dark, magnetic eyes and took the stool in front of him.

I closed my eyes making myself ready for whatever might happen. I hoped I could get some help for the physical condition that had plagued me after the trip. I had pain and a series of blood clots in my left foot. The doctor had diagnosed it as phlebitis. He had recommended ice packs and anti—inflammatory medication. <u>But,</u> the blood clots kept recurring.

My eyes were closed: I felt <u>HEAT</u> over my head. I <u>FELT</u> something like a burning, hot sun over my head. Then the heat moved over the perimeter of my body: I assumed the heat must be coming from his hands—as I heard him move from the back to the front. Then he placed his hands on my neck—on my back. The heat <u>ENTERED</u> my body. I felt peculiar as the radiant energy coursed through me. I would not have been surprised if I had turned to see aliens, so foreign was this feeling: this exceptional experience. Wherever his hands moved the energy flowed. Swirls of energy entered my feet and limbs. I was being <u>penetrated</u> by a gigantic force of energy. My mind slowed, and I became extremely tranquil. And finally, he whispered, "Go with God." Where was my seat? I vaguely recall returning.

I never retrieved my candle: it flickered in the holder the least of my concern.

Maggie, who had returned to her seat, said, "Are you alright?" I am sure my eyes were glazed: that I looked at her in a very incoherent manner. We sat for a few minutes, or was it longer than a few minutes? I had no conception of TIME. I sat trance-like while whirls of energy surged through my body. (Donald Zanghi later confided to me that he had just come from a class on Reiki healing, and that I was the <u>first</u> person his channeling had ever healed with the Reiki method). And so that evening was memorable to <u>him</u> the healer, and <u>me</u> the recipient.

"Let's go," Mag said, noting my state of body and mind. I think she feared I could collapse and what the heck to do with me then. I went before her, Zombie-like, from the temple. "What happened to you?" she inquired as we headed home.

"The heat, the energy <u>entered</u> my body. Mag, it is still there. I just want to get home <u>and</u> go to bed. I just want to sleep."

And I slept like the proverbial baby that night. The next day I felt nothing unusual—planned a dinner for relatives, fed the furry five, and life went on. However the next evening I was reading a magazine, with the TV blaring in the background, when I experienced a strange, tranquil feeling. My back was suddenly extremely hot. I felt the whirling healing energy in my torso <u>AGAIN</u>. I dropped the magazine, slipped into a quiet state of mind—might as well go with the flow. The energy whirled back and forth in my chest and abdomen for what seemed several minutes. I couldn't believe it: the energy had actually returned or had been there ready to reactivate. When I returned to a state of normalcy I called Mag to relate the experience.

The following day, sitting in the same chair, the experience happened <u>again</u>. This time the energy centered in my left hip, traveled down my left leg, and centered in the painful, (phlebitis) left foot. And I thought, Oh, God, maybe, maybe!

AND FROM THAT MOMENT ON I HAVE NOT HAD ANOTHER BLOOD CLOT IN THAT FOOT.

I was so amazed, I couldn't wait to see the healer Donald Zanghi, to relate the incidents. When Mag and I went for refreshments the following Sunday (after church) I stopped him as he passed—coffee cup in hand.

"My foot is better, so much better since the candle-light service! And the healing energy returned twice during the week," I exclaimed.

"Sit with me, tell me about it," he said. Mag and I joined him at the table. He seemed very interested in the return of the energies. "If you feel you have really experienced a healing—write a letter and I will keep it in my files. We always want to know of the healing experiences." We chit-chatted: there seemed to be a special spark of communication. Ah, the charming Italians, I thought. I had heard he was married and there were five children in the family. But I never saw any of the family at the temple.

"I can't begin to tell you how astonished I was at the candle light service when I actually <u>felt</u> your hands over my head, when I actually <u>felt</u> the heat." He smiled his energetic smile—at least <u>he</u> had known it was happening. "Well," I joked, "little did I realize I would be wearing your handprints on my back all week long." I promised to let him know what results I had. So far, so good, I had not had a blood clot in the foot all week!

Mag and I stayed for the mediums readings. And wouldn't you know, the medium turned his eyes towards me. He asked me if I had known someone who had passed to the spirit world by the name of Susie? And I said yes. "She is here with someone and they are together laughing. Her message to you is to get up off your duff and do what you are meant to be doing."

On the ride home I told Mag, "Susie, for God sake's, Susie!

She disliked me intensely. She was Dad's <u>second</u> wife. She disliked my Mom and felt the same way about me. Whenever she saw me she got ill!' 'Mag laughed in disbelief.' No, I'm <u>serious.</u> She was a diabetic and whenever I went to Saratoga to visit them she would take one look at me (a reminder of Dad's first marriage and my Mom), she would literally go into one of her diabetic reactions. Dad would sit her down, and pry her mouth open to get something sweet like orange juice into her system."

"Oh, no, Mag said, "you really <u>did</u> make her sick."

"Oh, I used to dread going there. But I felt such a duty to my Dad—for him to see his grandsons—that I'd brave the trip about once a month and endure Susie's dislike." I put my hand to my mouth at a sudden disruptive thought. "What a joke! What a cosmic joke—if we might have to come back after passing to the spirit world to guide people we were really hateful to."

"Oh, I'd better be careful of what I think of my co-workers in that case," Mag said.

"You know that message—'You'd better get up off your duff and do what you are meant to be doing,' really sounded like something Susie would say to me—and exactly the way she would say it." I began to ponder it. If this was a real message from the other side, what was I supposed to be doing? Did I have some kind of mission? Was I supposed to be doing some special kind of work? Hey, I was retired—what new project was I supposed to come up with? Was it something in relationship to other people—Mag, Doris? Peter? My sons?…Mom? I know I had felt so restive lately, so useless, so valueless. But WHAT was I supposed to be DOING?

The next Sunday we sat with Donald Zanghi again at the grove refreshment table. "Guess what, no blood clots in the foot. I'll give it a month or so and then I'll consider writing that letter. Certainly a healed foot is a healed foot."

He had some mini cheesecakes on his plate. "Where did you get those; I didn't see them." I asked.

"Ha, you missed them, hurry up there and you just might get one," he instructed. I got the last two; he still had four on his plate. "Oh, those were scrumptious," I said lapping up the last bite. He had one morsel on his plate.

He held it tantalizingly in front of my face. "Do you want the last one?" he inquired waving it in front of my nose. I could have killed him—I wanted that cake so badly. I pushed his hand aside.

"We all know the piggy that wants it," I retorted, Why did I feel so comfortable with this man. Barely knowing him, yet able to banter in this manner. Did I have a special connection to him because he was my healer? What had I thought? <u>He</u> <u>was</u> <u>my</u> <u>healer</u>.

YES, I BELIEVED I HAD A HEALER—THAT HE WAS THE CHANNEL THROUGH WHICH GOD HAD ENTERED MY BODY AND HEALED MY FOOT.

3

I study healing

Mag and I were up early the following Sunday—it was to be our first adult lyceum. (Sunday school class) I felt butterflies as I approached the Andrew Davis building. I hoped we wouldn't be put on the hot seat—I hated to be called upon in an unfamiliar group. In one corner of the room, chairs were arranged in a semi-circle. I saw a few familiar faces—part of the Cassadaga group: Rev. Ben Thomas, Rev. Sam Nickels and Don Zanghi. Others were chatting, perhaps 20 people. Mag and I said our hello and found a seat.

The Rev. Ben Thomas as moderator welcomed us, a prayer was said, and the speaker introduced. The Rev. Sam Nickels was to give us his ideas on <u>healing</u>. After my recent experience with a healing, I was literally all ears. Just how did they do this? What special rituals were important? What did the healer <u>feel</u> when they healed you?

Sam is striking in appearance and manner. He has a wonderful shock of white hair and wears a perpetual look of sweetness on his rather handsome physiognomy. When Sam speaks, you feel as if he is talking to you—in a living room setting. You are relaxed and "at home." He told us that healers are channels for God's healing. The healer must have a calling to help others. That the healer's EGO can be a stumbling block. <u>One</u> <u>must</u> <u>forget</u> <u>ego</u> <u>and</u> <u>become</u> <u>the</u> <u>channel</u>. Healer must be his conduit. The healer must 'Let go and let God.' But it starts with the healee wanting to be healed. The person realizes <u>he</u> must be brought back into balance. The National Association of Spiritualist churches has set certain guidelines for healers. Each healer has his own methods, but in the temples guidelines are kept. There will therefore be no messages, no prescribing, no diagnosing, and no special touching. The public ritual may be different than what the healer would do in his own home.

I let my mind take that a step further. If you had a bad heart you certainly wouldn't want a healer to put his hands in that direction! So I could see where the guide lines were important. "I feel pretty much at home here, don't you?" I asked Mag. Sam was now going to demonstrate a healing. One of the circle was chosen as the healee and sat on a chair—eyes closed—in front of us.

"We first let the healee know we are here, by placing hands on the shoulders," he said, so doing. "I let my hand pass above the back one, two, three times and over and above the front 3 times for healing of body, mind, and spirit. I say to myself that I am here and I wish to work with you. I pray to God, as I touch the shoulders, 'Guide us to greater light and healing. I feel the energy near her. I tune in to <u>energy</u>. We are trying through the energy to make the body harmonious. People are like little radio stations—they need to be <u>tuned</u>. People are like a crystal set; we are a fluid. Our crystals are our glands, such as the pituitary. Healers don't block the chakras: we <u>attune</u>. Then I put one hand on the forehead (area of the 3rd eye), and scan and attune sick areas with the other hand. I take 3 deep breaths, take her hands and say BE YE HEALED. And I tell her thank you and God Bless."

Sam finished with a special poem on Healing:

HEALING IS:
A lifelong journey into wholeness
Seeking harmony and balance in one's own life,
in family,community, and global relations
An instant of transcendence-above and beyond the
self Embracing what is most feared
Opening what has been closed,
softening what has been hardened into obstruction
Creativity and passion and love
Seeking and expressing self in its fullness;
Its light and shadow, its male and female

Remembering what has been forgotten about
connection,
and unity, and interdependence
among all things living and non-living
Learning to trust life.

Mag and I walked towards the temple. "Our first class," I exclaimed. "I feel different than I felt with any other Sunday School class. With other classes I secretly disagreed with what they were trying to shove into my mind, but here I felt I was learning something of the truth. I'm learning that probably anyone can heal. That the healer is only an instrument. These healers here are simply opening themselves up to God's love and passing it along to others. Isn't that surprising? They really aren't people with unusual gifts, just people who are <u>open</u> to God, and who want to <u>help</u> others," Maggie's eyes glowed with agreement.

My sister and her husband came to dinner Monday evening. We take turns with dinner invitations, and Mom, Doris, and I all consider ourselves good "Adirondack Mtn. cooks." I made a meatloaf, mashed potatoes, and a salad. I baked a lemon pie from scratch: one of my sister's favorites.

Doris helped put the food on the table. "My feet are killing me. It hurts to walk. Why don't these doctors have the tests that can diagnose what I have? Why do I have to keep suffering like this?" She walked gingerly on her tender feet. She also has an aneurysm, and swelling in her joints. She <u>did</u> pose an enigma to her doctors.

We called Jay, her husband, to the table. "Perhaps you should come to the Temple for a healing," I suggested. Her problems were more than medical. They are consummate buyers and consequently in debt; she constantly worried. Jay was a diabetic, and a Southern gentleman. Her Northern culture often collided with his Southern culture. Perhaps there could be a healing of <u>body, mind and spirit</u>.

As she ate the lemon pie, she exclaimed "Oh yummy. I'll try to get to Cassadaga. Maybe it would do me some good."

The following Sunday I decided to try another healing from Don, as I, too, had multitudinous problems including a damaged vertebra (car accidents) and a diseased heart. Don had one person after another, so by the time I got there the lecture had already begun. I was so nervous, I thought every eye must be on me, as I was practically the only person left to be healed. I felt the energy radiating from his hands. My skin glowed from the warmth. But I could <u>hear</u> the lecture. I was so distracted the warmth, the energy didn't seem to <u>penetrate</u> as it had before. I returned to my seat, and realized I had <u>blocked</u> the energy—it had only gotten skin deep. I had not been receptive. When I saw Don the following Sunday I explained what had happened. "Oh, yes," he said, you can block the energy by being unreceptive. But have faith, maybe some of the energy is lying dormant." There was much laughter at our table. I knew Mag related to Don too. There was some emotion here I couldn't identify. I looked at Don and knew there was something afloat I couldn't really define.

The next Sunday I was more than ready for the next Lyceum class about healing. After the classes on healing there would be classes on other topics. Ben Thomas wanted to know what we as students would like to study. It was all so new to me, just about any topic they chose would be agreeable to me. This time, Ben gave the Lecture. He explained that every healer has his own techniques, but still must work within the church guidelines. He also explained certain things obstruct healing. If you don't love yourself and others how could you heal? If you had hate in your heart how could you heal? Healing takes place where it should (in body-mind-spirit) and SPIRIT knows where it will be directed. Also, a healer needs to be in good health himself, eat nourishing foods, etc. And it is true, that some healers work better with certain people. I thought of Don and how I had gravitated towards him and considered him my healer. There has to be an attitude in the healee of wanting to be healed. The healee may not feel anything at the time, but get latent results. Ben had to leave as he was giving the lecture at the temple. So Don Zanghi and Ann Smith led a discussion with the group. We discussed that there must be receptiveness on the healee's part. Of course, I had to relate my latest experience where I became so nervous, so distraught that I had blocked a healing. Ann said we don't really need to "feel" the healing, that it can lie dormant in us for a time. Another gal told of the healing of her migraine headaches.

It was said that SPIRIT will not let us down as the healer or the healee. Another woman said her pain got worse immediately after the healing procedure, but disappeared the following week. FEAR is a major obstacle to the healing force. Absentee healing (where the healee is not near the healer) can and does work. Your thoughts are powerful and you can channel God's love and healing to another. Healing may take a different form: it may lead you to the specific doctor you need to cure your condition. It was thought that getting permission to heal (such as absentee healing) is not necessary as God is in control and if the healing is meant to be it will happen.

I arrived home and found major illness. CC my Siamese cat had been ill for months. He had recurrent bladder-kidney problems. He had already had two operations. And he also had "running" fits and was on phenobarbital. God, the poor thing was so skinny, and just ate and drank everything in sight. I knew Doris thought I was wrong just trying to keep him alive, euthanasia, to her would be merciful. CC let me know about his problems. Oh, yes, indeed, he let me know. There was vomit in several places on the living room floor, he had wet on the sofa cover, and there was bloody urine in the bathroom sink. Oh, poor CC I thought, beginning to clean the mess. "You will be back at the vet's tomorrow."

CC and I were at the vets the next morning. Doc Leo looked at his chart. "I have to do a couple of tests. You say he eats and drinks excessively."

"I'm not kidding, he drinks and eats more than all four cats combined. And <u>he</u> is the one wetting up the litter."

"He did have the diabetes test two years ago and it was O.K., but I'll rerun it."

CC and I talked, as the rather long tests were run. CC is a talker and responds when spoken to in his low gutteral tone. The doc returned and leaned against the cabinet. "He is now a diabetic."

"Oh, no, what does that mean for him?"

"Well, it's certainly not good, but many owners give their cats the insulin injections."

"I'm such a ninny, such a chicken about things like that, unlike my sister who once owned horses and even gave them medication shots. Oh, God, CC."

"Look, I think you can do it. And it must be done if you want him to live. But we will have to keep him here for a week, or longer in order to regulate the amount of insulin he will need."

I squeezed CC, I certainly couldn't put him to sleep—it looked like I had to control my squeamishness. "You may think I'm odd but I go to the Spiritualist church in Cassadaga and I put CC's name in the prayer book. Lots of people are praying for a healing. And you know, I may take a healing class so I can learn something about healing—maybe I can do it."

"No, I understand," he said. "I did a lot of meditating in the past. In fact, I began to get very sensitive to people and animals through the meditation." And so I left CC at the animal hospital, knowing, I too, must do everything in my power to help him.

And as if an answer to a prayer: a bulletin was in the church on Sunday. There would be healing classes taught by the Rev. Jane Hall beginning the following week. It was a bit intimidating for me (who was I to think I might do something the mediums could do), but I signed up.

Therefore at seven o'clock on a Monday evening I once again began a "Journey to Cassadaga." I was alone in this one (Oh, Maggie where are you—working)! I thought the class was at 7:30, but found the church yard crowded with cars. That was all I needed-to be late. I walked to the open door, about 20 people were seated, and the Rev. Jane talking. She motioned me forward. A group of strangers—no, I spotted Mr. and Mrs. Gates and then from the front row smiling broadly, Don Zanghi. I went to the healers desk (yes every eye was on me). I felt my face flush in embarrassment. Don came to the desk to say hi and handed me the envelop I needed for my weekly payments. I think he realized I felt discomfort.

I found a seat beside the Gates (who live in Cassadaga), and Rev. Jane continued reading from her handouts:

"What is Spiritual healing?"

"Spiritual healing occurs when the unseen forces provide extra power which rides on the vehicles of the healer's own magnetic force. This positive energy affects the spiritual body, which in turn affects the cell-consciousness and chemistry of the physical body, It can help you physically, mentally and spiritually."

I certainly was aware of that truth. Physically my foot had been healed. The energy had stayed with me and I was sure my attitude towards life was improving. I no longer felt useless.

"What is a Spiritual Healer?"

"A Spiritual Healer is one who, through his mediumship, is able to impart vital, curative force to pathological conditions. He works in conscious cooperation with spirit beings called guides."

Well, I'd have to see about that one!

"Who heals?"

"The healer doesn't do the actual healing. The doctor doesn't heal. The God-spirit working through the healer and the patient's body intelligence heals. The healer and the doctor provide the proper conditions for the healing to take place."

I guess most people might feel that the healer is the channel for God's healing energy; I'd agree with that.

"What makes a Spiritual Healing most effective?"

"Attunement in vibration between healer, spirit healer and patient is necessary. As a patient, the important thing to remember is to be relaxed and receptive, mentally and physically. A negative attitude toward life builds a wall around you which is difficult to penetrate with healing force. You can only absorb as much healing force as your mental and corresponding physical state will allow."

My first and second healing experiences with Don Zanghi were certainly proof positive of this. During the candlelight service I was relaxed and receptive in mind and body. The healing energy glowed on my skin and penetrated me in great swirls of healing. But the second time I was nervous, distracted, distraught both physically and mentally and the energy was blocked from actually entering my being.

We were about to do a group meditation, but before we began we read the following:

The Great Invocation

From the point of light within the Mind of God
Let light stream forth into the minds of men.
Let Light descend on Earth.

From the point of Love within the Heart of God
Let Love stream forth into the hearts of men.
May Christ return to Earth.

From the center where the Will of God is known
Let purpose guide the little will of men-
The purpose which the Masters know and serve.

From the center which we call the race of man
Let the Plan of Love and Light work out.
And may it seal the door where evil dwells.

Let Light and Love and Power restore the Plan on
Earth.

Rev. Jane took us on a guided mediation. She led us into a garden of many flowers. She told us each flower color had its own vibration. We were to see (with the 3rd eye) and be aware of each flower and its color.

I could see the garden and its flowers in my mind eye. And after our garden trip I felt relaxed and peaceful.

"How many of you could actually feel the difference in the vibrations of a red flower and a yellow flower?" She asked. Many raised hands, but although I could visualize in the meditation, I did not "feel" the vibrations of the flower colors.

The class was dismissed with prayer. I found Don outside. "I couldn't feel the vibrations of the flower colors." I complained. "How can I really expect to do this—I'm not like you mediums who have studied and seem to have some kind of special powers."

"You don't do it: you are the channel and <u>Spirit</u> <u>does</u> it. Anyone can channel spirit if he lets the love flow through." I said good night, still feeling unworthy and filled with doubt.

Maggie was curious as to my opinion of the healing class. She settled down on the couch holding Tiggie by the paw. Rev. says we will become more and more sensitive with each class. But I felt like such a failure when I couldn't <u>Feel</u> the difference in the color vibrations. Now <u>you</u> don't visualize well, so maybe you would be the one to <u>feel</u> the color vibrations.

"But you <u>could</u> see the colors?"

"Oh, yes, the colors were very vivid during the meditation. And I was very relaxed. Gee, maybe she is right, maybe I will feel more as we go along. But, I have all sorts of doubts that I will be able to channel healing.

"You are still going to try? To go to the next class?"

I flipped Bear-Bear off my lap. "Oh, I'm determined," I said with a sigh.

Rev. Jane greeted us the following Thursday and handed out a paper that hit me where I lived. She certainly touched on my <u>FEAR</u>. It was called <u>Attitudes</u> <u>in</u> <u>Healing</u>. She read from the papers—"There are 2 basic Emotions—LOVE AND FEAR. They cannot co-exist. Make self feel Love when Fear creeps in—fear goes and we will not feel the pain of it. What I <u>choose</u> is a reflection of what I <u>felt</u>. I choose between Peace or Conflict—Love or Fear. I have the Power to choose."

Well, there I had my problem. I had a <u>fear</u> I couldn't heal like the mediums do. I had to replace the feeling of fear with love. Whenever I felt the doubt and fear I had to replace it with love—just feel God's love instead.

Then she read from <u>Spiritual</u> <u>healing</u> 11:"Spiritual healing comes under one heading—LOVE—you must have self love, not ego—as well as love for others." Matthew 5:24, "Love your enemies".

Matthew 7:1, "Judge not least ye be judged". Accept others where they are in life, not where <u>you</u> want or think them to be.

KNOW—What you think is what you create.

KNOW—What you think you make into being.

KNOW—What you think is what you make manifest.

What you send out in thought form is what you receive back to you. It's like a boomerang. You are the creator. Now you may wonder what all of this has to do with Spiritual healing. You must clear yourself of the negative aspects of your life of doubts, fears, guilts and angers of the past and present in order to let the healing energies come in and heal. You must say 'I of myself can do no healing-I am an instrument of the Divine Force working through me.' The healing takes place between the subject and the Divine Force."

I felt like a bell had rung. What was I so worried about me for? Why was I so concerned with my feelings? What was the purpose of healing? Well, it certainly didn't have much to do with my little ego—and I guess those words verified that.

We took a break and I looked around at the group: attorneys, nurses, a retired minister, a computer programmer, some of the Cassadaga group—and me the retired writer and teacher. I wondered if some of them felt uncertainty like me—the attorneys perhaps? I gleaned from the discussions, that several of the nurses were already into healing. I began chatting with a nurse who had rushed from work at Daytona to attend the class. We began to discuss meditating (she did it, too), and cats. She had a cat that weighed 32 pounds. Now that made my Tony at twenty-five pounds a light weight.

"Do you notice your cat annoying you when you meditate?" I asked.

"Yes, the cat keeps putting his face near mine, and seems to want to be close," she admitted.

"My teacher said the cats know you are tuning into a higher plane and they want to be a part of it. That you should really not be in the same room with them as they will disturb your meditation," I laughed. I remembered the first time I tried to meditate near my five: Tony was on the back of the chair, CC on the arm, Bear—Bear was trying to get into my lap, and the others were rubbing my feet. Yes, cats disturb meditation!

When we returned, Rev. Jane again read from some handouts. "Remember you are a Spiritual Being here for a human experience not a Human Being here for a spiritual experience. Atmospheric conditions and much that is not known may cause some of the variations as to the quantity, quality, and effectiveness of the healing force. Practice and experience will increase the results just as in other professions and more can be done. Everyone has some of this Force. Life depends on its effectiveness and would be impossible without it.

Have a non-judgmental attitude—accept others as they are—not as you want them to be. Everyone exists to be loved—not judged. Also do not condemn self. Forgiveness is the key to happiness. When I see you guilty-I am reinforcing myself in guilt. 'Judge not, lest ye be judged' (Matthew Ch. 7, VI)."

She held up a child's photo. He was ill and in a Florida city about 100 miles North. "We are going to form a prayer circle and do an absentee healing," She informed us.

I felt some trepidation, but joined the circle. One person sat in the center of the circle with the child's picture between her hands. We held hands and started sending healing thoughts to the child. Two of the people in the circle were touching the healers (Jane's) back and she in turn touched the back of the person with the photo. "The healing energy is building," she said, "I feel it." Apparently the energy went faster and faster around the circle as we sent healing thoughts and held hands. I felt no actual vibration in my hands, but swayed as I felt a little dizzy. We continued to hold hands and ended the healing session in group prayer. Somehow, I felt the healing had reached the child.

Outside, I caught sight of Don. "I bet you felt the energy vibration, didn't you?" I knew his smile meant affirmation. And once again, I felt like I had missed the boat.

I returned home to find CC sick again. It wasn't due to diabetes—but the recurring bladder problem. He was vomiting so I couldn't give him a pill—just had to wait it out until his body fought it off. I cradled him—poor baby—and I hadn't even learned how to give him a healing yet. He was so really precious about his insulin shots. I was using operant conditioning. I always gave him a special treat after each shot. So when I said "Do you want your shot?" He would scoot down on the kitchen floor and wait for the dreaded needle. Then he would bound back up for his special treat—stand right by the frig and really meow for the forthcoming treat. So, CC and I learned to live with his maladies. But daily I wondered if I was doing the right thing—would he be better off in the spirit world? Was I being selfish keeping him here?

Hallelujah, I was going to get another opportunity to learn about healing. There was a workshop on Healing by Rev. Steve Hermann, an ordained minister, certified medium, and healer through the National Spiritualist Association of Churches. Steve had lectured, demonstrated clairvoyance and conducted classes and workshops throughout the United States and abroad. Very impressive—maybe <u>he</u> could inspire me.

I walked into the Andrew Davis Building and was quite amazed by Steve Hermann: I had heard he was thirty-something, but he looked like an amazing young, curly-dark headed movie actor. But when he spoke he spoke with the wisdom of the ancients. Strange to hear such knowledge coming from a face that looked like a young angel. We sat in a circle (about 15 of us including Don Zanghi). For the first part of the program Steve spoke profound truths about healing. We could question at any time.

He told us healing was really simple—not as complicated as people want to make it seem with the rituals and such. He said it is nothing more than <u>compassion</u> and <u>love</u>. The healer is just the channel. I told him of my experience in a healing circle—that I didn't feel the energy vibration traveling around the circle. He told me not to concentrate on the RESULTS. I laughed and said, "Oh, you mean <u>I</u> have to get out of the way?" And he smilingly affirmed the healer must get himself and ego out of the way. We must feel God's (Christ's) healing power and open self to it—let it flow through you to another. It can be in the present or absentee healing. You simply pass the healing energy through you. But, you concentrate on doing it and never let your thoughts stray. The healer must not be tired or ill—then he is not a good channel for the energy. The healing may not show up immediately—it can lie dormant and work at a later time. It can be a healing of body, mind and spirit. Spirit knows where the healing is needed. I know he spoke of much more during the hour, but these thoughts stayed with me.

We took a break and I walked outside thinking, "I get in the way—I worry about what I feel—I have to think of Christ's love and power, I have to feel his love and power and simply let it flow through me to another.

When we returned, Steve had us sit in a meditative prayer circle for a guided meditation. We held hands, Don on my left, a woman on my right. As we prayed, I felt tremendous energy between Don and me—but not with the woman on my left. Later, Don called to inquire if I had felt the energy—indeed, I had!

After the meditation Steve asked us individually about our experience. Some people had seen spirit guides, some went deep, but actually saw nothing. I saw my "writing" guide angel (who is most mischievous), and another who was more dignified. We enjoyed sharing our guided meditation afterthoughts.

Next, Steve said, "Rub your hands together. Now place them facing each other (the palms), and you can feel the energy you generated." Yes, I did. Then he said to rub hands together and place them near a partner's hands. Yes, the energy was there again.

Finally, we got into a really keen experiment in healing. He chose our partners. One person was to sit in a chair at one side of the room and think of a negative experience. Across the room a partner was to fill her heart with God's love and move slowly towards the partner in the chair. When the person in the chair "felt" the love coming towards her she was to raise her hand. Then hands were placed on the person's shoulders to transfer love.

I sat in the chair and felt all the negativism I felt that morning with CC's illness. Suddenly, I got a nice, warm feeling, and I raised my hand realizing it was coming from my partner who was slowly walking towards me (from behind). Then she put her hands on my shoulders and I truly felt better, as if she were taking away my negative feelings. We related our experience to the group. Next, my partner sat in the chair, and I walked forward, trying to send love. But, she didn't raise her hand. I focused on love, Christ's love, as I put my hands on her shoulders. And yes, she related she did feel my energy enter her body. I was afraid she hadn't felt it, but she did!

Following this, we did a "laying on of hands" healing. One person sat on the chair and the other healed. I sat on the chair and a woman, who was already a healer, put her hands on me. I could feel her energy as her hands passed over my head and back. Later, she sat in the chair and I said the prayer for healing, got into God's healing energy and placed my hands over her head, around her body, and finally on her shoulders. When questioned by Steve, she said she felt a lot of energy and when I had placed my hands on her shoulders she could feel the energy enter where she had had pain.

At last, at last I had put me aside, and had tapped into Christ's healing power. Yes, anyone could do this just as Christ had promised. You could heal with the love and compassion of God. You could be the channel for the love and the healing. I felt profound gratitude.

Steve gathered us in a circle. "We are going to form a close circle and to the tune of Amazing Grace we will sing a verse of 'I AM' and then a verse of 'WE ARE'." We all gave each other individual hugs and meeting.

I walked out and my heart was singing, singing "I AM."

The next morning I put CC on a chair. I knew this was a very sick, perhaps terminal, cat, but I wanted him to benefit from healing energy. If nothing else, perhaps it would ease his pain or calm his valiant spirit. I said my prayer to God, and made myself receptive to the healing energy. I placed my hands on CC and let the energy flow through me. I concentrated on the healing energy. I knew CC felt something because he became restless. "There," I told him, "I will keep trying, and maybe, no, it <u>will</u> help you."

I knew that I, too, could benefit by the laying on of hands. Each morning I suffered from extreme fatigue. I was so tired a trip to the grocery store was akin to climbing a mountain. How long could this damaged heart keep beating? Was it worsening?

On Sunday, I headed for Don Zanghi's healing hands. When he placed his hands over my head the energy was so potent my skin glowed. He placed his hands over my ears and the heat was so intense it was actually like smelling the odor of electrical wires burning. He placed his hands on my neck, and then my back—great waves of energy entered my body. I vaguely remember returning to my seat. I went into a meditative state: I just wanted to feel the energy in my body. I didn't want to hear or see anything. I longed to escape to some dark corner and simply feel the energy. It was marvelous coursing throughout my body. Maggie kept saying my name. I heard her as though from a long distance. She touched my hand. "My God, you are radiating heat," she whispered. "Heat is just flowing from your whole body." I knew she was right—the energy was in and around me. I thanked God.

For several days I "felt" the healer's handprints on my back. After much further study I now realize what I felt was the healing energy stored in my heart chakra. Many times I would automatically go into meditation and the heat would flow over the entire back.

My blood pressure is usually high in the diastolic or high in the heart rate (pulse). But after one of my meditations (where the energy flowed down my back) the readings were all in the normal range.

I was no longer fatigued—no longer spent half the morning on the sofa, too tired to move. My energy has returned and I once again feel like a normal human being.

I reflected on my Journey to Cassadaga and know that spiritual healing is a most important gift. And the gift had been given to another and that gift had been used to channel the healing energy to me for my body, mind, and spirit.

4

Can I believe in Mediums

Suddenly it was <u>November</u>. It seems the older you get the faster time slips by. Was it <u>August</u> when I first journeyed to Cassadaga? But for anyone who thinks (as I used to) Florida is all one perpetual summer and that seasons do not exist—WRONG. From July to September you swelter under a blanket of heat. One does not have to tell you of the first day of summer, you step outside (perhaps late June) and are in dense suffocating heat. Now, native Floridians hale the day, luxuriating in the scorching rays of the sun. But, we transplants always dread the first real day of summer—as it foretells the long, long, long, hot summer—the interminable days of 98 and 99 and 100 degree temperatures of ultra high humidity. The nights do not cool to any appreciable degree. So you jump from air-conditioned house, to air—conditioned car, to air-conditioned store, to air-conditioned church: namely Colby Temple.

Mag and I made our way to Cassadaga. The country-side now looked different. Foliage was dried and withering. Flowers were of the red or purple hue rather than the delicate springtime hues. "I'm so glad November is here," I said. "I can <u>breathe</u> again: the air is more like September air in the Adirondack Mountains." Mag was always warm, going bare-legged in 30 degree weather, so I know she agreed with me.

At the temple we sat through the guided mediation and the lecture. Finally, it was time for the readings, and we were to be aware of what we were wearing as a means of identification by the reading medium. The lady in the black hat with the flowers on the front? Oh, no, <u>me</u>. I answered with my name, as mediums liked to hear your voice. And this time his message was on the material side. He said I couldn't do everything I really wanted to do, because of money. He related that I would come into money, so that I could travel as much as I desired. He said that money would no longer be of any concern. When we walked towards the grove and refreshments, I said, "Mag I know you just believe everything that the mediums say will come true, but I just am not sure yet. I'm not sure they are really communicating with the spirits on the other side. Maybe they have very active imaginations and just visualize the whole thing. I want to believe it, but I'm still filled with doubts."

"Oh, I've believed they can do it—right from the beginning," she replied. We walked under the magnificent trees towards the Davis building. I wondered where she got such faith in the mediums. We had both read in the annual program about the difference between a psychic and medium: "Everyone is psychic. It is our sixth sense. Some individuals develop this ability to the extent that they are capable of tapping into mental vibratory energies and providing clients with information pertinent to their mundane everyday existence. A medium is an individual who possesses vibratory energies capable of merging with spiritual energy thus enabling the medium to bring information and assistance to their clients of a higher edifying quality. It is higher in the sense that the information does not come from mind or mental energy but rather from a God source of information. All mediums are psychic, but not all psychics are mediums. A medium is also referred to as a Spiritual Counselor."

The Annual also explained a seance: "The term seance is an antiquated term referring to a group of people usually sitting around a table in a darkened room. We no longer practice seances as sensationalized in the movies. We now have circles more commonly referred to as psychic and spiritual development classes."

I read further concerning a Reading: "A reading is a term for what we also refer to as spiritual counseling." I now knew that at some point I must choose a medium and have a private reading: I must really see for myself what this was all about. I read further: "These services are obtained from your Spiritualist minister or certified medium. We believe in the continuity of life and communication with those who have made their transitions. Our mediums communicate with spirit, not necessarily those whom you have known on this earth plane. We have the natural law of attraction and because of the circumstances you are experiencing, a spirit may be attracted to you because they will be for your highest and best good. A medium may bring in a relative/ friend who has made their transition, but no guarantees can be made." I thought of the medium who saw Susie beside me. Susie, a woman who had married my Dad and who had not liked me, but now gave me advice from the spirit side. I read further," Spirit people wish to help, guide, direct or confirm what may be going on in your life but not to control, you have free will and are in control/command of your own life. Spiritual counseling is achieved using the ability of the medium's mind. The use of the psychic sciences such as palm reading, tarot cards, etc. will not be employed." I wondered how many people thought of the mediums as fortune tellers rather than a channel for the spirits. It answered, "We do realize the validity of these psychic sciences; however, our organization does not advocate the practice of these sciences on our grounds. In our attempt to educate the public and become more professional in our approach, we realize that the general public may view such practices as fortune telling and since we are not nor have we ever been fortune tellers, we do not encourage the use of these tools. All mediums in our organization work as mental mediums." Well, I thought, that should really put fortune telling to rest. Unfortunately the general public did not have the Annual and most people I met did associate the Camp with just that. "Demystify spiritualism" this book introduction stated. But first I had to demystify mediumship for MYSELF.

I thought of some of the mediums who taught at the lyceum. I thought of them as highly intelligent people: I respected them. Therefore, if I respected them, did I think they were playing a hoax on people? These, indeed, were, most sincere people, and I realized "they" believed in what they did. Now, I had to investigate to see if "I" could believe.

A division of Daytona Beach Community College (a scholars anthology project) had researched the mediums and had their photos and biographies on display at the Davis Building. I took special note of a few of them one Sunday after lyceum.

Rev. Lillian Weigel: "Lollie was raised in a small Pennsylvania town settled by her grandfather, who came from Prussia. All little towns had hex doctors. One came to her home when she was four years old and said she would be important: she was born with a psychic gift. Another psychic black woman told her she would be a psychic reader in the future. Lollie says psychics are a dime a dozen, but there are really good mediums in town." I have seen Lollie at the lyceum, and she is a very sweet and dignified lady.

Rev. Jerry Frederick" Jerry lives in Daytona but rents space in Cassadaga. He came to town to be healed (bad back and kidney stones). He believes God took care of him because he did not have to have surgery. He spent his early years on a farm in Wisconsin. During that period he left his body (astral projection), and it scared him. But no one told him it couldn't be done—so he just did it. When he realized that astral travel was not what everybody did and that it was supposed to be impossible—it took him 25 years before he learned to do it again." I have heard Jerry at the temple when he gave illuminating lectures, and I have heard him at the Grove giving readings.

Rev. Donna Bohrer: "People get used to meditating at a certain time and a certain place each day—the body gets used to the rhythm of this. Spirit is like a thought in your mind. She works in the public defenders office in Lake County. Her coworkers think what she does at Cassadaga is just fine. I heard Donna speak at Lyceum—she has a keen analytical mind.

Rev. Jim Watson: Jim spent a lot of time looking for religion. He was born in Eustis, Fl. He came to Cassadaga and the first thing he remembers is a sense of freedom and he felt comfortable and kept coming back. Physical phenomenon is coming back as part of Spiritualism. His spirit guide came in through a trumpet that floated towards him and made his presence known with a loud greeting—'White Bear Ho'. It took months in group meetings to get the trumpets levitating. But it is amazing when you see it. When it faces you-you can feel the energy on your face." A levitating trumpet? Now, that I would like to see!

Rev. Nick Sourant: "The Rev. Nick, and the Rev. Jean Sourant live in one of the oldest houses in town (from the early 1900's). They fixed it up, and art work from all their travels (especially the Southwest) fills their home. Nick was a field engineer for thirty-five years. He has studied the White Brotherhood, Egyptology, and alchemy. In regard to our culture and our lives—he asks the question—what has caused all this? The answer for Nick is <u>thought</u>. Thought meditation can control high blood pressure and mental health. Nick can drop his pressure from 98 to 78. Mediums can tune in to spirit guides that go to an infinite type of intelligence that is beyond our wisdom. Spiritualism gives us proof of continuity of life." I have heard Nick speak formally and informally at the lyceum. I admire his intellect and sweet gentle manner. Because Nick is a true intellectual I am prone to believe what he says. This is a man of science (engineer) who believes in the spirit world.

Rev. Janie Henderson Owens: "She has always been an artist, drew faces. Now she does spirit drawings. She draws whenever she sees spirit guides. She actually does readings from her drawings. Some of her paintings are about past lives."

Rev. Arlene Sikora: "When she was six years old she kept seeing her grandmother who was already in spirit. Her parents called her visions nightmares. Under pressure, she said she was hallucinating and she sent grandma's spirit away. But she was lonesome for her and called her back several years later. Arlene had come from a Catholic background, but became a spiritualist in 1972. She taught physical education in Massachusetts. Later, she did academic counseling which she said actually was like giving readings. She was a Reverend in a Massachusetts church for fifteen years. But the snow sent her to warmer climates. Now she resides at Port Orange, and has her office in Cassadaga."

I walked out of the lyceum into the cool November air. I saw Don Zanghi headed towards a car driven by a young, blonde woman. He smiled and got into the car. I knew instinctively that this was his wife. Just the type this charming Italiano would be attracted to, I thought. But as I gazed at them riding away I knew that if I saw them walking down a street together I would never think of them as man and wife. Well, enough of <u>those</u> stupid thoughts, I said to myself, as I went towards the Temple. And wouldn't you know when the bulletins were handed out there was one for a Sunday afternoon class, Nov. 24th, on Spirits and Spirit Communication taught by—Don Zanghi. If there was one person that I had complete and total faith in—it was Don. So, I wanted to know more about Spirits and Spirit communication and I could believe what Don had to say. I decided on the spot to attend that class.

As usual, I felt out of my element as I walked into the Davis Building on Nov. 24th at 2 p.m. I didn't really <u>know</u> anyone in the group—I recognized some of the Cassadaga people, but only had a <u>nodding</u> <u>acquaintance</u> with them. I paid my fee and went towards the coffee urn. As I poured the coffee and picked it up, the door attendant came up behind me to remind me to sign in. I was startled, and the slippery white plastic cup fell to the table, splashing hot coffee in every direction. Don was setting up equipment, and laughingly called out, "You sure made her nervous," And I felt like the proverbial bumbling fool as someone brought numerous paper towels for a clean-up. For someone trying to be inconspicuous I had gotten off to an auspicious beginning.

A couple of tables housed chatting people, but I took the table near the front. After Don's helper finished helping, he took a seat directly behind me. Don must be an omnivorous reader—the front table was covered with books. He would not be making a presentation unless he had read every book.

We were to learn that spirits tried and did communicate with us through, tapes, radio, television and a machine called a Spirit Com. I was actually going to <u>hear</u> some of these voices. Don spoke lucidly and with authority. He <u>believed</u> in everything he was about to tell us. So, maybe, finally, I, too, could believe the mediums really did talk to Spirit.

I first heard messages on <u>tape</u>. The experimenter was Sarah Estep. She asks questions of spirit, pauses, then replays the tape. She used the tape, mike and earphones. It is called EVP (electronic voice phenomenon). The messages I heard were rather garbled. One message was perhaps from an alien world as they said "We're cruising down." In answer to a question Sarah asked," "How did you find me?" The answer was "I found the link." And when Sarah asked "From what world do you come?" The answer was "From the center of Theos." They called ice "thick water" And they told her "We're here next to you."

Also using <u>tapes</u> was Mark Macy, the president of Continuing Life Research. This is a group of researchers that believe Spirit is trying to break through to us using I.T.C. Instrumental Transcommental. They are working with people like Thomas Edison (on the Spirit side). Sometimes the Spirits appeared in suit and tie. Why? Because our thoughts create our reality. If the person had appeared that way on the earth plane then the Spirit appears that way so we will easily recognize them.

With <u>radio</u> one needs to get an open station, and the spirits use the white noise to emulate a voice. One voice said that the use of drugs here could hurt you when you got to the spirit world. Another voice spoke of the many levels of heaven.

There were also <u>TV</u> images. Some people might think those were a hoax. The TV messages say that everything is the same on the other side: homes, mountains, rivers, etc., only existing at a different vibratory rate. One message said, "You are in a carnal body—only after metamorphosis will you be closer to the truth." In one segment a mother recognized the voice of her son who said, "I'm waving to you." One TV image said we live in our "etheric" body 3 days after death, then go to our astral body. (Frederick Jergenson recorded over70,000 voices.)

And then we get to Spiricom a machine built by man, but built under the supervision of spirits. It uses a radio frequency generator and receiver. Thirteen tones are used for the spirit's voice. The voice that comes through is very deep and robot sounding. The person who invented the machine was George Meek who had an engineering degree and was once advisor to Averil Harriman. He founded the "Metascience Foundation." He did ten years of work looking for electronic proof that the mind and personality survive death. And through the Spiricom machine communicated electronically with the dead. A worker, O'nelle, communicated with a Dr. Muller, in spirit and felt a field of energy in the room. The Dr. was very authoritative in his tone.

After Jeanette Meek passed O'nelle was able to communicate via the Spiricom with her. She gave a message to her husband, Greg. She had their dog in the spirit world with her.

And so our lecture ended with thanks from Don for our attendance. I left the building feeling like I had had a visit to Mars. Spirits, real spirits talking through the TV, radio and machines. November 24th and I felt confused as I rode home. But Don had presented this, and I believed in his intelligence. I made the turn towards home feeling my world had expanded—it was more than the fading leaves in the darkening twilight sky, it was more than the people I loved and touched and had communication with—it was this world and other planes—perhaps almost superimposed on this plane—existing at a different vibratory rate—it was my world of reality (or illusion) but perhaps a world that could be visited by spirits that had passed into those other planes. My head reeled with all those thoughts as I neared home.

December came to Florida. Not as it does in the North-with chilled winds, darkening skies, and flurries of snow. No, it came with glory to us transplants: it came with sunny skies, lowering temperatures, and lowering humidity. Now we could breath again (warm, not torrid air), and enjoy a ride in a convertible. My world went on, but with a difference. I was no longer the August (pre-Cassadaga) person without goals, without a zest for life. I now looked forwards to classes at Cassadaga, the lyceum, the Temple. I was once again a student. I gloried in being a student. Maggie and I loved our Sundays at Cassadaga beginning with the Lyceum, the temple, then to the Grove service (with all the goodies in food and conversation), then on to a lecture. And it seemed every time I was interested in a particular subject there was a lecture or service to enlighten me.

I read in the Sunday bulletin of a Candle-light Medium's service. I was still searching, searching to believe without a shadow of a doubt in the Medium's abilities. Don's lecture had gone a long way in the way of scientific proof. But, I still required more subjective information.

I telephoned my sister and Maggie and we collectively decided to attend the evening candle-light service for a reading. It was dark outside when Doris and I arrived. The beckoning candles glowed in the Temple windows. We paid a nominal fee at the door and received our numbers. We visually drank in the dimly lit temple, and feasted on the air of tranquillity and harmony. Several tables were set up for the eight or ten Mediums. I could see two in front, two at the front corners, and several in the back. I didn't know what medium I would get! I felt <u>God</u> would choose for me. Doris said, "I'm the first of our group and I have these high heels on. I hope I don't fall on my face walking up there." The floor in the Temple is rather sharply pitched and I sympathized with her—but I had worn low heels. Maggie was late—coming from work in Ormond. She finally slipped into the seat next to us: she would be in the set of numbers following us. People were now called in the first set of numbers. They were instructed to light a candle, place it in a holder, and return for it when their reading was completed. Two people ushered them to available tables in the front—and then others to the back. My sister was nervous, and sat quietly while Maggie chatted about her work and various trivia. I looked back and could see the mediums deeply engaged in conversation with their clients. If wondered WHO I would get.

Excitement now made my knees weak. Doris lit her candle and was ushered (Oh, no, up the <u>steep</u> <u>incline</u>) to a medium at the side of the building. I didn't dare look to see if she made it or was flat on her face! I lit my candle and put it in the holder and turned—to pass Don Zanghi's table. He smiled a warm smile as I passed. He already had someone moving towards his table. I returned his smile and shrugged my shoulders as I went past him and was directed to the back of the church to the table of—Margaret Ann Larson.

She had her eyes closed and took my hands in hers. As I sat down, she was silent for a few moments and then talked very rapidly for several minutes. I leaned in close to catch every word. "I feel you are very artistic—that you will soon be doing something in the artistic field. It is something to do with letters, words, writing.

"I see it, this writing, coming up like a whirlwind from the ground. I think it will happen in February or March.

"You will have help. You have a spirit guide helping you. In fact as you sat down—she was near you—I caught a glimpse of her skirts as you sat. She is dressed in a long flowing gown.

"I see you with a book or a manuscript. You will be traveling to New York—or somewhere, a city—. I see the book or manuscript under your arm.

She asked if I had a question and I told her I had been a writer and that of late I had had no inspiration.

As I returned to my seat I thought, "This is December and she said I would be writing in February or March. And a book!"

I hoped she was right, but was doubtful. At the moment I was a writer without a word to say.

Doris had returned. "I almost slipped when I went up that incline," she exclaimed. "Was your reading good? What did she tell you?" she asked.

"Yeah, if it was good I'll try to get her too," Maggie chimed in.

I related what Margaret Ann had said. "It sounds wonderful, too good to be true, that I might have something to write about by February. I really can't imagine what it could be—but if it comes true I'll certainly have faith in mediums," I said.

"Oh, I'm going to try to get to her, too," Mag said. And sure enough her number came up next. I saw her light the candle, and the attendant motioned towards a corner table, but Mag ignored her and marched right up the aisle to Margaret Ann's table. "Leave it to Maggie," I laughed to Doris. "And what was your reading like?" I inquired.

"Oh, nothing as exciting as yours," she said. "I told her about Armond's death and how I mourned him and that stuff about the strange occurrences after his funeral."

"You mean about opening the door of the house and the scent of roses being all through your house. And how he always gave you roses: they were your favorite flower."

"Yes, I told her that, and that it had happened several times. And I told her how the bed corner just went down like someone was sitting on it that one night. Oh, I told her all this after she told me that someone was there with us—perhaps a husband that had passed."

"Oh, you mean she told you Armond was there with you tonight?"

"Yes, she related he said he was so happy that he had gotten through to me after he passed to Spirit. She also said it is hard for spirits to communicate like that—it depletes their energy.

"Oh, Doris I would have freaked out—Armond was right there with you tonight! Oh, God, Doris aren't you just freaked out?"

"Well, yes, but she didn't tell me anything about Spirit guides or a career like your reading."

And I thought—"Oh, my God Doris, your husband was right beside you tonight!"

Maggie returned to her seat. We were curious and she told us, "She said I was like a semi—truck traveling in the fog. It is like I'm crawling slowly along and don't really know where I am going. She thought I might go back to school—maybe in the field of accounting. And that I had a child's spirit." I thought of Mag and how she did face life with a child's spirit—she was for the most part laughing and outgoing facing the world with wide eyes, not really seeing the harsh reality of events. She refused to look at her weight problem—the problem that was really harming her whole existence. But her sales were great—she charmed her customers with laughter and jokes. And I always thought she was capable of doing something more satisfying than the telemarketing sales with which she seemed content. Now, this medium had told her more schooling was her answer. I wondered if that would inspire her.

I was so intrigued by the reading that Margaret Ann had given me, I decided to call another medium and have a-one-on-one paid (longer) reading. I selected the Rev. Helene Liberte.

Yet another journey to Cassadaga. I wondered if this trip would once and for all prove that mediums could contact the spirits. I stopped near a small weathered building where Helene gave her readings. She greeted me (she is a tall, large—framed woman with a warm smile), and ushered me on to a screened porch waiting room.

She later beckoned to a small "reading room." She began with a prayer for healing, fulfilling needs, and invited those in the spirit world and guardian angels to attend the reading, and she asked for clear, wise choices. Helene asked for a personal object, and I handed her one of my bangle bracelets. She twisted the bangle round and round and grew thoughtful.

"I don't know where it is in time, but I see you attending a male—you are taking care of someone.

"I took care of my ex—husband before he died of cancer."

"He came in as soon as I touched your hand. He wants to tell you of his appreciation for what you did while he was terminal: he was in and out of a coma at the end, but he knew. Was he very protective of you? He is sending the message for you not to be naive, not to look at the world through rose-colored glasses. In whatever you do, look at the whole picture."

I could believe Winston, in spirit, was here because I often felt his presence while riding in the car. And yes, he was very protective of me.

"Jeanette, I see you up at three or four o'clock in the morning, is this right?" This seems to be a very productive time for you: you are full of creative energy then."

I laughed. "Yes, I do get up at four o'clock and read books on Spiritualism, and do some writing."

<u>She</u> laughed, "Well, it looks good on you, <u>I</u> couldn't do it, but you can make some wise decisions then."

"Does your mother have a chest condition? I feel a heaviness there. But she has amazing hardiness. I think you two argue because you have the same energy. You are very close. She gets younger as the day goes by, and has a sharp mind."

How right she was about my near ninety-year-old Mom, who lives alone, and amazes everyone—in spite of a heart condition.

"Is the name Myra or a name with an MR in it, close to you?"

"Oh, my Aunt Muriel, he (her husband Ernie, in spirit) called her Murlie."

"He wants her to know how much he appreciated her. He is such a loving person, I'm getting such pleasure from his energy."

"Have you been to the doctor's lately?" I told her of an upcoming heart echocardiogram. "I see a procedure. But your Uncle Ernie assures me he is checking it and he will have it work in your favor."

"I see a piano. Did someone in spirit love classical music?" And yes, I had an Aunt Anna, reared in a convent who played the organ and piano. "And I feel your grandmother who had some arthritis. She lived a long life. Her message is to keep fluid and you won't have her problems." My Grandma lived to be 92. "I see a J—some one is telling you J is here.' He is sending much energy towards you—especially around your birthday. He will be helping with publishing of a book. He is a loving person." I thought, Oh, <u>Dad, Dad, Dad</u>. "He (Joseph) tells you your Mom will be ill around the holidays, but she will recover.

"I see you with books, books, books. You are really exploring. The more you get the more you want: you want TRUTH. You are remembering, remembering. You went through the mundane in your life and now it is click, click, click. It is very important to apply the truth you learn. You have very healing hands."

"You are going to visit the Southwest. You are being drawn like a magnet. It will be prior to 1999, you will be going with someone. The trip will have a spiritual aspect."

We hugged good-bye and she handed me a tape of the session.

AND ONE OF THE FIRST SUPERNATURAL EVENTS HAPPENED. WHEN THE TAPE WAS PLAYED TO ME THERE WAS A THIRD VOICE GIVING A SUGGESTION. WHO THE VOICE BELONGED TO AND WHAT THE MESSAGE WAS WILL BE REVEALED IN A LATER CHAPTER.

And so the veil was lifted: I believed in mediums.

5

What Spiritualists believe

At the Grove, the following Sunday, Maggie and I sat next to Donald Zanghi. "Did you finish that letter about your healing experience?" he asked. I told him I would complete it for the following Sunday. And later, as we all walked towards the door he casually mentioned, "You know I've moved to Cassadaga. I live right here now."

"How wonderful. How lucky you are to be living here in this rarefied environment," we both exclaimed. Outside, Mag and I looked at each other.

"Do you think he is bringing his family here? I never see them here, why would he move here and bring them?" Mag pondered. And I wondered if he had moved here alone—if there was discord in the family. I wondered—and my heart felt stuck in my throat.

I heard the next lyceum lessons would be on the declarations or principles of the church. This was the basis of the Spiritualist religion and I needed to explore it. In the <u>Annual</u> there were "commonly asked questions" about the religion. "Do <u>you believe in God</u>? Yes, we often refer to God as infinite intelligence. We do not believe in a personal God. Infinite Intelligence means to us an all pervading mind and intelligence that is in and of all things animate and inanimate; a dynamic and creative force and power that governs all things by immutable and unchangeable law."

I wondered what my Mom would think about that. I guess she believed in a more personal God: one that would personally reward her if she were sin-less and punish her if she sinned.

And the question Mom would certainly have asked, "<u>Do you believe in Jesus?</u>" Yes, We consider him the greatest teacher and medium that the world has ever known, a God-man who knew and applied the Spiritual Law to a greater extent than any human soul who had ever lived, and we hold his name sacred in every way." Well, I knew that would not answer <u>all</u> of my Mom's questions.

"<u>Do you believe in the Bible</u>? "Yes. We understand that God truth has been given to mankind down through the ages and that these truths have been recorded in books known as Bibles." The Bible is up front on a special table in Colby Temple.

"Do you believe in the devil? "No. We consider evil as the negative of good. All God's creations are good. God could therefore create no evil. Evil is good misunderstood and misapplied by man. We do not believe in a personal God and therefore cannot believe in a person devil." Mom has been battling the devil all her life—I wonder if she would be disappointed to know that she had been tilting at windmills. So many people seem to have a <u>need</u> for evil personified.

"<u>Is witchcraft or black magic part of Spiritualism?</u>"

"Absolutely not." I have seen nothing that smacked of witches or magic at Cassadaga. These people are normal, intelligent human beings with whom I am honored to have an association.

"<u>Do you believe in Heaven and Hell?</u>" "Yes, but not in the traditional sense. They are not places or abodes but rather states of consciousness. Heaven and Hell can literally be experienced right here on earth." I have learned so much more of Spiritualist beliefs at the lyceum. For instance Spiritualists believe through the 8th principle that the doorway to reformation is <u>never</u> closed to any soul who desires it.

"<u>What is natural Law?</u>" "Natural Law is the law which God set in motion to govern all creation. It is immutable and unchangeable. In working with spirit, many ask how we know that we are not dealing with an evil spirit. Those who seek communication with evil in their hearts can attract to themselves evil, lying spirits. Those who seek communication with loving, sincere, wholesome, constructive counselors, asking only the highest and best from the God source, will only attract likeminded spirits. This is Natural Law. Specifically, the Law of Like Attracts Like. Religion is essentially right living, and is attained by a knowledge of God's Law that teaches us to understand our relationship to the Father/Mother God and the Brotherhood of Man. The golden rule is its precept. Religion is not theology; religion is not dogma or creed, nor is it necessarily related to any particular church, minister, priest or rabbi."

"<u>What is a reading?</u>" A reading is a term for what we also refer to as spiritual counseling. These services are obtained from your Spiritualist minister or certified medium. We believe in the continuity of life and the communication with those who have made their transitions. Our mediums communicate with spirit, not necessarily those whom you have known on this earth plane. We have the natural law of attraction and because of the circumstances you are experiencing, a spirit may be attracted to you because they will be for your highest and best good. A medium may bring in a relative/friend who has made their transition, but no guarantees can be made. Spirit people wish to help, guide, direct or confirm what may be going on in your life but not to control, you have free will and are in control/command of your own life. Spiritual counseling is achieved using the ability of the medium's mind. The use of the psychic sciences such as palm readings, tarot cards, etc. will not be employed. We do realize the validity of these psychic sciences; however our organization does not advocate the practice of these sciences on our grounds. In our attempt to educate the public and become more professional in our approach, we realize that the general public may view such practices as fortune telling and since we are not nor have we ever been fortune tellers, we do not encourage the use of these tools. All mediums in our organization work as mental mediums."

"<u>Does Spiritualism recognize other churches or religions?</u>" "We emphasize the fact that there is good in all religions. Truth is truth, whatever form it may be presented in and right living is the keynote to all religions. Religion is the process through which you recognize, understand and demonstrate your spirituality. Spirituality, living your belief or understanding, is a way of life, not something applied only on the Sabbath." I really like the emphasis on living your religion on a day to day basis.

Now I knew what other people were curious about concerning Spiritualism. But my curiosity concerned—the precepts upon which the religion was grounded. I had had a difficult time with the healing concept, a difficult time believing in the mediums—and I wanted to learn more about each individual principle of the faith. The lyceum would provide the answers.

At the next Grove service Mag and I sat beside two men we recognized as regulars. I was talking to Mag when I heard the name Don being discussed by them. I have to admit my ears did purposely pick up the conversation.

"Yes, I heard Don had moved out here too."

"What's it all about—a divorce?"

"Well, I was joking with Don." I said, 'I heard you are living out here—what does this mean a divorce?' You know I was being facetious. But, he answered—'Yes, a divorce'."

I turned back to Mag and continued our conversation-but I don't remember a word I said to her.

And I went to the next lyceum and looked across the room at Don. Stop pondering, I thought, give your full attention to Dr. Harold Warren (giving the overall view of the principles). Harold Warren has a Doctorate in metaphysics. He touched on all nine of the principles or declarations:

1. We believe in infinite intelligence "We may add the word—'God' to the declaration because people have difficulty with this principle as people have been taught God was in the form of a person and we are in His image. We teach God is infinite—in everything."

2. <u>We believe that the phenomena of nature, both physical and spiritual, are the expression of infinite intelligence</u>. "Nature <u>is</u> an expression of infinite intelligence. It has a precise course, like evolution, etc…"

3. <u>We affirm that a correct understanding of such expression and living in accordance therewith constitute true religion</u>. True religion makes us understand the universe and ourselves. Natural laws are laws of the universe, of physics, and spirit. There are thousands of these laws. For instance when certain conditions exist—certain things happen (like tornadoes). The laws are there; science slowly discovers them.

4. <u>We affirm that the existence and personal identity of the individual continues after the change called Death</u>. "The individual goes on after death, continuous with individual identity, ego and soul. The spirit world is developed into different planes (many mansions). We have the same character as in the present life. Talking to spirits happens all through the Bible."

5. <u>We affirm that communication with the so-called dead is a fact, scientifically proven by the phenomena of Spiritualism</u>. "There is variation in communication with Spirit. Even professionals can have problems as the spirit consists of a finer basis (vibrations). We all have a psychic basis. When you have a personal experience <u>that</u> is your proof. Thousands of people have these psychic experiences.

6. <u>We believe that the highest morality is contained in the Golden Rule: "Whatsoever ye would that others should do unto you, do ye also unto them."</u> "Jesus restated the Golden Rule, but it existed long before Christ. It is a universal truth. The positive or negative comes back to you here or in spirit."

7. <u>We affirm the moral responsibility of the individual, and that he makes his own happiness or unhappiness as he obeys or disobeys</u>

Nature's physical and spiritual laws "The individual makes his own way as he obeys or disobeys the natural laws. We have personal responsibility. You make the decision—you are not a robot. If we make wrong decisions—it may be a growth experience."

8. We affirm that the doorway to reformation is never closed against any human soul, here or hereafter. "Catholics do believe in prayers for the dead. And the Bible does say Jesus descended to lower realms and saw people there. In spirit we can be ignorant, but we can make changes. The doorway to reformation is never closed."

9. We affirm that the precepts of Prophecy and Healing contain in the Bible are Divine attributes proven throughMediumship. "The Bible speaks of angels and prophecy. as Spiritualists say that prophecy continues."

This (condensed) was Dr. Warren's overall view. And I knew that in the weeks to come the declarations would be analyzed for us. I knew we needed in depth study on each principle, and I was ready. Not only did I need to understand the details for myself, I needed to know more in order to answer the questions others would ask when they discovered I attended Colby Temple.

On the way home, I was uncommunicative as Mag did her usual dance with the traffic. Would Spiritualism be MY religion? Much of what I discovered was already in my heart. I kept reorganizing truths that were "shocks of recognition."

And then there was Don Zanghi. Why did I think of him so often? Was there a "shock of recognition" here too?

I was very quiet on the journey home.

Joyce Marie Harvey led the lyceum for declarations 1—3 (the deeper analysis). This woman's warm smile adds sunshine to any lecture. We started with (1) We believe in infinite intelligence. She spoke of infinite as being without bounds, extending without end and intelligence as perceiving meaning, ability to adapt to new situations and ability to understand complex matters. "In <u>Conversations with God</u> we learn that words can sometimes be inadequate—there is a higher communication. We are part of that which is ever present and ever active. Spiritualism has been recognized for 150 years. We do make changes and contemplate adding—God to our first declaration.

If people don't see the word God they perceive it as something else."

From a handout by Rev. Ben Thomas I gleaned the following knowledge: "Spiritualism recognizes this Source in a greater scope of awareness in that "God" cannot be limited to an anthropomorphic being but must be all inclusive, omnipotent, omnipresent, and manifesting through all forms of life and matter. What is meant by not believing in a personal God is that God is beyond our ability to clearly define in terms available to us in our physical reality. Any attempt to define the God Force limits it and therefore becomes a false statement.

"Spiritualists do believe that Infinite Spirit (God) is in charge and in full control of all living and existing things. Natural Laws are the rules of operation for all existences and evolutions everywhere, all the time. It is Infinite Spirit's way of true fairness for all. All is happening within Natural Law. God does not reach down and amend the Law for anyone, anywhere, anytime.

"It is believed that all of humanity, all of creation is being moved ever forward equally by the power of Infinite Intelligence (God) towards higher awareness. No one is held back other than by their own choice, or cast out of the plan. God's grace is shone equally on all. It is only our own inability to perceive it or our lack of awareness of it, not the supply of it to us that is lacking. Spiritualists believe that they are responsible for their own actions, good or bad, not an external powerful entity. To be allowed to say 'Oh, the devil tempted me and I gave in', is to not take responsibility of the consequences for our own actions. We are always responsible for our actions!"

"It is equally irresponsible to give God all the credit when we do good. If we do this we are not aware of any spiritual growth we made by bringing these virtues into action. God has no hands on this earth but ours, no feet on this earth but ours, no lips on this earth but ours and no eyes on this earth but ours."

Joyce reviewed the second principle, <u>We believe that the phenomena of nature, both physical and spiritual, are the expression of Infinite Intelligence</u>. "We think of the <u>phenomena</u> of nature as the physical and spiritual expression, and <u>expression</u> as on going action of God. <u>Phenomena</u> can be the outcome or showing of nature. Look at the <u>expressions</u> in nature and see God. Spiritual expression is important in this physical existence."

And from Rev. Ben's handout: "Does God ever change or alter, even temporarily Natural Law? No, God is impersonal and we are all responsible for our own destiny and decisions. God will not alter the Laws to shield us or anyone else from the consequences of our own actions.

"Infinite Intelligence (God) is in and through all things. This principle expresses our belief, as Spiritualists, in the pervading presence of Spirit in everything and everyone. All people are a perfect expression of God's creation and are all equal in the eyes of Spirit. Infinite Intelligence pervades and controls the universe, is without shape or form, is impersonal, omnipresent and omnipotent."

"Andrew Jackson Davis gave us spirit communication that has helped greatly to give us our idea of evolution and natural law. Our idea of evolution and creation is that natural forces guided by natural law, influenced by spirit influence, are guided towards a definite goal, rather than by chance circumstances as put forth by science. This change or evolution continues even in present day. As we follow a more spiritual path we are constantly accelerating our natural evolution as is our choice. We believe, as Spiritualist, that the Infinite Intelligence has, down through the ages, created all forms of organic life through a marvelous system of evolution, all worlds and all life, both material and spiritual, being governed by the divine rules called Natural Laws.

Joyce continued with the third principle: <u>We affirm correct under-standing of such expression and living in accordance therewith consti-tutes true religion</u>. "You incorporate this in daily life. <u>You walk the walk.</u> <u>You are faithful to the truth</u>. We incorporate the principles into our lives and we live them."

And from Ben's notes: "It is very clear that a correct understanding of universal order and life in harmony therewith is the underlying pur-pose of all religious systems and it is calculated to help advance human progress. As man understands the laws of nature (NATURAL LAWS OF THE UNIVERSE), the laws of God, he can better cope with day to day living. Understanding is necessary for compliance. Therefore, we can do the right thing at the right time if a clear explanation is given and understood. A correct understanding provides the way for a correct expression of the idea and thus produces obedience of the law.

"In keeping with Spiritualism's stress on personal responsibility the for-going statement puts the decision for personal growth where it belongs, in the hands of the <u>individual</u> themselves.

"Our Third principle sets the course for non-interference with other religious systems, as we realize <u>all</u> are guided by the Divine and Natural Law and require no interference from us.

"Only in this manner can correct understanding come about. An individual can only make progress along a spiritual path by personal decision, reached by a period of reasoning and deduction. Any other method generally brings about a changing of ideas according to the atmosphere they are currently in, with little commitment to stay the course they have just chosen. The opposite of this is blind fanaticism: total and complete commitment without reason."

After the lyceum we went to Colby Temple for the services. I saw Don in the back of the church ready for the healing ceremony. I looked across the parallel aisle and saw…. his wife and the whole fam-ily. Mag nudged me and looked across at them. Why hadn't I seen them before? He was supposed to be getting a divorce—why all of a sudden—was the entire family in church? I looked across at them—the tall, blonde woman and the children: ranging in age from perhaps eight to sixteen. And I had heard they were all her children from previous marriages. Imagine instant fatherhood to five children! Well, that had to be some kind of man to take on that responsibility. And rumor had it the divorce was <u>her</u> idea. Don finished the healing ceremony and took a seat beside them. Was this a reconciliation? My heart ached for him and I wanted whatever would make this man happy. I still stared in that direction and he must have felt my gaze as he turned, looked into my eyes,and gave me the "Zanghi" smile. I sat for the remainder of the service confused.

At Lyceum, the Rev. Barry Braddock led the discussion for declarations four, five and six. (4) <u>We affirm that the existence of the personal identity of the individual continues after the change called death</u>. Barry expounded: "We are of electrical and magnetic energy flows. Wherever you place your attention—that's where you will be—if on a spiritual plane. It's like surfing the internet—you can get what you need—as long as your motivation is OK. Alexander Graham Bell really was working on the invention of the telephone in order to communicate with the <u>spirit world</u>. Spirit guides bring you information—they are there when you need them."

More information was provided from Rev. Ben Thomas's notes. "We never die. Survival is a fact. There is a natural body for the purpose of expression on the physical plane. As the soul takes a physical body at birth into this world, likewise it sheds the denser body for a more refined body (spiritual body) at the time of transition into the realm of spirit. Our personal identity, our character, continues to express itself after the change called death. We are basically the same after the change as before the change. We don't suddenly sprout wings and become angels—or devils. It is not the purpose of Spiritualism to attempt to convince stalwarts of other faiths to change their beliefs, rather to provide accurate and understandable answers to those who come seeking.

"After the spirit has severed its relations with the physical body, man's moral status is the same as immediately before the change and he enters into a high or low estate according to his attainments in this world. By a subtle law both the good and the evil he has done are fairly weighed; he himself holds the scales and renders his own judgment in The Hall Of Judgment. The unfoldment of his mental, moral and spiritual faculties is continued indefinitely by processes not unlike the manner pertaining to this world. (N.S.A.C. MANUAL Pgs. 40—41).

"Man is a three-fold being, material body, spiritual body or soul, and spirit. In Spiritualism, there is a definite difference between the soul and the person's eternal spirit. The soul is the "body" or that which is a vehicle for the divine spark or eternal spirit. The soul is also sometimes referred to as the intermediate principle as that more closely describes its function, which is to act as a medium between divine spirit and the physical world.

"In orthodox belief, the soul and divine spirit are considered to be one and the same.

"The soul is built, so the philosophy of Spiritualism teaches us, of the very finest emanations of the food we eat, the water we drink, and the air we breathe, and ifs growth is affected by every act, thought or word of our earthly lives. It is a replica of our material body and, at the time of so-called death, withdraws from that body and functions through eternity as the house of the spirit.

"It cannot be said that the soul is devoid of matter, but it is a much higher and more of a spiritual refinement than of that which we contact on the earth plane. Spirit, of course, is the very highest vibratory rate, far beyond our material conception." (1; THE FUNDAMENTALS OF SPIRITUALISM).

My mind drifted to last Sunday's church service. The answer to the Donald Zanghi enigma seemed to have been solved. Joyce Marie was the lecturer, and in the course of her address she mentioned that Spiritualists really tried to "live" their religion. She looked directly at Don and said that even people who were getting divorces treated each other with dignity and respect. Don was grinning broadly and I knew he had accepted her accolade. And I thought, yes, yes, yes.

My mind was pulled back as Barry continued with the 5th declaration: <u>We affirm that communication with the so-called dead is a fact, scientifically proven by the phenomena of Spiritualism</u>. "Communication is like the speed of light. But we must still our own personality to receive it. Yes, we can block the energy from higher places. We receive it through faith—or grace.

From the Rev. Ben's notes we learn more about the fifth principle. "After our transition to the Spirit World, we continue to express ourselves through scientific demonstration of mediumship, it has been proven that communication between the earth and the Spirit World is a reality."

"A spiritualist endeavors to mold his or her character and conduct in accordance with the highest teachings derived from such communication. You don't have to be a medium to be a Spiritualist, only believe in the proven fact that communication is done."

"We teach and demonstrate the existence of this belief, not ask it be taken on faith. This is where the scientific part comes in, in that this can be demonstrated anywhere at any time by scientists and investigators from all walks of life, enough to convince anyone who is open-minded."

"The Spirit world is a natural state of existence, originated and sustained by natural law; including many varied conditions or spheres corresponding to the variant intellectual, moral, and spiritual planes of inhabitants. At physical death, each human soul passes into a condition in correspondence with its degree of unfoldment, ethical and spiritual; and, under the law of eternal progression, through continued aspiration and effort, it is destined to outgrow its imperfections, and ever increase in goodness, knowledge, wisdom and happiness as the endless ages roll."

"The agents through whom the Spirit-world communicates are called mediums, and may be classified as follows: inspirational speakers and writers; test mediums, or those through whom direct personal messages come; mediums who heal the sick through spirit aid, physical mediums for the production of objective phenomena; and various other classes of mediums through whom are produced many other manifestations of physical and mental planes."

Barry shuffled his papers readying himself to expound on the next principle. My mind turned outdoors to the late November day. I would have to compose my holiday baking list. Jam bars I thought. I always placed them on the top of the list. My sons would gather from New York State and Florida and their Mom always baked Jam bars, Toll-house cookies, sour-cream sugar cookies (frosted) and fudge. And then there was the Christmas card list and all the letters to enclose along with them. The presents were in the closet—bought throughout the year. Oh, dear, it suddenly felt like such a monumental ritual—when the only thing that was really important about it was what would be said in the next principle.

"We believe that the highest morality is contained in the Golden Rule, 'Whatsoever ye would that others should do unto you, do ye also unto them'." Barry read.

"The rule points the way to harmony, peace and happiness. What goes around comes around. Our 'higher self' can help with problems. Emotions are about 75% of our energy. Energy is power. We learn to become more powerful."

The Rev. Ben's notes on this principle were, most enlightening. "Spiritualists clearly reveal their understanding and expression of ethics by the Golden Rule. This guiding principle is a thread echoed throughout all major forms of organized world religions since the beginning of recorded history. This proves the Spiritualist's assertion that truth is periodically brought to the earth plane equally for all of all faiths and cultures. Truth is constant throughout the ages.

"When practicing the Golden Rule, good for evil, we are overcoming, by choice, all basic instincts of self preservation and allowing our true spiritual nature to rule. This act is the ultimate in the struggle to attain enlightenment as it is the struggle of our animal instincts against our higher self. Our instincts are very automatic as a rule, whereas our spiritual side must be consciously brought out. As our path continues we begin to have the spiritual side more automatic and less driven by emotional reactions.

"As is clearly seen the Golden Rule has changed little, if any through thousands of years and hundreds of translations. (Quoted from the N.S.A.C. Spiritualist Manual The Philosophy of Spiritualism pgs. 39—41)

"In the spirit world man retains his individuality, the unfoldment of his mental, moral, and spiritual faculties is continued indefinitely by processes not unlike the manner pertaining to this world. Good deeds springing from a good heart have a creative force in building pleasant abodes in spirit life, and conversely the opposite create their own unhappy habitations. Everyone must compensate for all unjust or unkind deeds, here or hereafter and attain a state of justice before they are prepared to enter upon the path which leads to spiritual happiness and progression. There is no death bed confession that allows this natural law of compensation and recompense to be circumvented. We, as Spiritualists, do not hold with the theory of Vicarious Atonement."

"Spirit communication is not meant to help avoid life lessons or avoid life's consequences, only to help understand these more clearly. Many become disillusioned because of failure to warn of some impending doom. Spirit will stand back and allow us to do it on our own, otherwise we could fail to learn the lesson properly. The main purpose of spirit communication is to prove the continuity of life after death, delivering the message that there are no dead and there are no dying. We also hope to live a more moral life from such communication.

And from Ben's notes I had to add this because of the truth and sheer beauty of the words: (N.S.A.c. SPIRITUALIST MANUAL-ROAD TO HAPPINESS pgs. 107-108) "Would you be happy while you dwell on earth? If so, pull up the thorn trees from the garden of your life and plant in place thereof the myrtle trees of affection. Then will your days be filled with sunshine and your paths be paths of peace-

Would you daily bless your neighbors? If so cast upon the vibrating ether tender thoughts of loving kindness daily, for they shall find lodgment in some heart—

"Do you long for opportunities to be good and great? If so, conquer self, master the unruly passions, cultivate the intellect and apply your powers for humanities good.

"And are you in love with life? If so 'know thyself', for in so doing you shall learn the laws which expand and prolong life and you shall perceive the nobility of giving no unnecessary pain to any living creature.

"Do you seek knowledge? If so, despise not the small things; deem nothing too sacred for honest investigation; sound the reasons for things, meditate upon the wisdom of the learned, but accept only Truth as the final authority.

"Are you in sorrow and in need of consolation? If so, go forth on some errand of mercy; minister upon the sorrowing; speak words of comfort to the distressed and the despairing, for thus shall you find what you impart to others.

"Are you distressed with thoughts of wrongs done? If so resolve to do wrong no more; open the windows of your soul and let the sun shine in; seek companionship of the good, ask for the aid of invisible helpers, and set yourself some worthy task.

"Are you satisfied with self? If so, learn from the truly great and good how small are your attainments, how crude your development; look into the starry heavens and learn to be humble; seek to answer the questions of a child and learn the limitations of your wisdom." These words of wisdom entered my heart.

Mag and I rode home in the sweet autumn air. "I've learned so much here, Mag," I told her.

"Can you believe we've only been coming here a few months; I feel like I've always been here."

Yes, it was like I had finally come home. I kept recognizing truth—here and the truth—there. I had come to grips with healing and the toughest one for me—mediumship.

And in Spiritualism you <u>lived</u> what you learned. I was trying hard to be kinder in my conversations with Mom—although she had the superb knack of rubbing me the wrong way. But I was making a conscious effort—really trying to avoid conflict.

Then there was Peter, my lover. I was really having second thoughts about our relationship. Was it time to close that chapter? Could I overrule the body passion I still felt? Something inside my heart tolled the death knell.

The Rev. Sandra Moore was to lead the next lyceum on the last three principles. "<u>We affirm the moral responsibility of the individual and that he makes his own happiness or unhappiness as he obeys or disobeys Nature's physical and spiritual laws</u>. She said, "I believe two things set Spiritualists apart (1) the continuation of the personality after death (2) We are responsible for our actions—we make our own reality. We create our own problems and challenges. We are in control of our lives. In other religions you may not have total responsibility. Thoughts create the emotions that follow. We have personal responsibility—watch your thoughts. It is really karma (laws of cause and effect). What you think <u>this</u> moment affects the <u>next</u> moment. You can change what you think about things."

The Rev. Wayne Hobson's handouts expounded further. "The philosophy of Spiritualism teaches us that we ourselves must make atonement for our errors or sins. What is sin? We are told in John 1, 3:4, sin is the transgression of the law. Therefore it is quite evident that if we break Nature's law, we commit 'sin' or error.

"The laws, of course referred to are Natural laws, God's laws, or Universal law. This teaches us personal responsibility. By understanding and abiding by Natural law i.e. the Law of Cause and Effect, Law of Friction, etc.; we can in effect guide our 'destinies'.

"So when these laws are 'broken', you cannot shift 'blame' or responsibility to another.

"Jesus the Christ understood the Law and lived in harmony with it. In Matthew 5: 17 and 18 we read: 'Think not that I come to destroy the law or the prophets. I have come not to destroy, but to fulfill'.

'For verily I say unto you, till heaven and earth shall pass, one dot not one title shall in no way pass from the law till it all be fulfilled.'

Later, in the same chapter, He identifies these laws as law(s) of the Father.

"Man—made laws change, atonement varies. God's laws, Natural laws, do not."

Sandra continued with the 8th principle. We affirm that the doorway to reformation is never closed against any human soul here or hereafter. I think this is my favorite principle because it proves we are a part of God and that he will never destroy us. We will always have the opportunity to reform on this planet or on the spirit side. Sandra said she was bothered about souls burning in hell—before she discovered Spiritualism (Well, Sandra, I didn't buy that either). "Everyone can change. Personality changes and grows here, and on the other-side. Spirits also help us," she exclaimed.

And from the handouts I learned, "Every day, hour and minute permits a new opportunity. Man can change his way of thinking, acting and living. Aware of the continuity of life, each person is afforded the opportunity of progression. However, progression may require the changing of one's habits. Eternal damnation had no place in the philosophy or religion of Spiritualism.

"To many Spiritualists this is the most beautiful of all the principles, for it holds out a definite promise to man that whatever his mistakes on earth, he is not eternally damned.

It removes that most destructive thought of fear and instills in its place the knowledge of our ability to make just reparation for all earthly mistakes and eventually work our way out of the darkness of sin into light of spiritual happiness.

"From <u>Spirit teaching</u>, a most excellent book derived through the phase of automatic writing, by Rev. W. Stainton Moses: 'We know of no hell save that without the soul; a hell which is fed by the flame of un-purified and untamed lust and passion, which is kept alive by remorse and agony of sorrow; which is fraught with the pangs which spring unbidden from the results of past misdeeds; from which the only escape lies in retracing the steps and in cultivating the qualities which shall bear fruit in knowledge and love of God.

"We learn that the Law of Reparation opens the doorway to spiritual progression in the heaven world." Amen, I thought.

At the Grove service Mag and I went through the refreshment line and Don smiled us over to his table. I looked at his plate and laughed. "A little hungry?" I queried.

"This, young lady, is breakfast and lunch, not brunch."

"No, <u>I</u> have the brunch," I laughed comparing my bagel and coffee cake to the mound of food on his plate.

I had handed him the letter concerning my healing the week prior. I knew student mediums found all such letters, certificates, etc., useful in their quest for certification. Don had been studying for <u>six</u> years—which meant he was a level 4 student, getting prepared for the certification committee. I looked at Don, I had never considered him in any manner but equal with the other certified mediums. I had attended his lectures, had seen him moderate services, had been healed through him, and had heard his readings. How could I consider this man of wisdom a "Student-medium?"

"I took your letter with me to one of my Reiki classes, and read it to them." I also had the Rev. Janie Owens read it."

"Woah, should <u>I</u> be flattered too?", I asked.

"Janie thought you did a good writing job, as well as giving the facts of the healing. And the Reiki people were also impressed."

I sat there eating my bagel, but I bet I just glowed.

At lyceum Sandra gave us the final declaration (9), <u>We affirm that the precepts of prophecy and healing as contained in the Bible are</u>

<u>divine attributes proven through mediumship</u>. "The prophecy and healing bring people comfort, knowledge and peace," she informed us.

And from a handout taken mostly from N.S.A.C. Spiritualist Manual and the Bible, "A simplified way of saying this declaration is 'God speaks to man and acts through man in the past, present and the future.'

"First we shall consider the gift of Prophecy and Mediumship. Prophecy has several definitions; (1) prediction of the future under the influence of divine grace; (2) act or practice of a Profit; (3) any predictions (4) something prophesied or predicted; specifically the divinely inspired utterance or utterances of a Profit. (5) gift of speaking under the influence of the Holy Spirit. The first and the fifth definitions explain more to the point what we in Spiritualism feel expresses how we work with spirit. Some of the Old Testament quotes include: Numbers 11:25-29, Samuel I 28: 7-19, Kings II 22: 12-15. Some New Testament quotes; Mark 9; 4, where Christ Himself converses with the spirit of Moses and Elias, Thessalonians I; 5; 19-20. As can be seen from these quotes, there were mediums of old and they were held in high regard. Most were counsels of kings and many helped to shape the world and society we now live in.

"It is the practice of Spiritualists to hold communion with spirits gone before for several reasons; (1) To learn from them moral lessons; (2) To receive instructions from spirits in regards to natural law; (3) To hold communion with our loved ones on the other side; (4) To prove the continuity of life after death by bringing back evidential and helpful information.

"Now to consider the gift of Healing. The most noted quote from the Bible comes from the New Testament, MATT 10; 1-5, where Christ bestowed the gift on his disciples. Healing has rarely been contested as a noteworthy gift from God to man and there is a renewed interest from many of the orthodox churches to re-introduce it into their services.

"A common claim from the orthodox is that the communing with spirit in the Bible was only with the Holy Ghost or God or angles not disincarnate spirits as we do. Not so as shown by Mark 9: 4, where Christ himself conversed with the spirit of Moses and Elias. As can be shown from Matt. 10:1 healing is also a God-given right.

And so my study of the declarations came to its conclusion. However, I am sure I will in the future, learn more about them. I am finding Cassadaga to be very God-centered. I found warmth and friendship from the residents. I feel "at home."

I will soon be writing my application for membership, at Colby Temple. I am asked why I want to become a member and I will reply, "I can now read the declarations with belief in their veracity. As a Spiritualist I have the desire to live my life in the light of these principles of truth and beauty.

6

Natural laws

My house was now filled with the aroma of holiday baking. I made the jam bars with the scents of cinnamon filling every cranny of the kitchen, cut them, and stored them in the freezer—one more item crossed off the baking list. The fudge was the most fun, because I had the most fun after it was put in the pan for refrigeration. It was the delight of sitting in front of the TV with a cup of freshly brewed tea and the cooking pot in hand—just sitting, sipping, and scraping the chocolate clean.

I had always loved the excitement of the holidays, the cooking, the family dinner, the decorating, the presents—ah yes, the presents. I had a closet full already. I bought continuously during the year. I did hate shopping during the season I never had the patience to wait in long check-out lines. So, I just bought off-season. Except for my man, Peter. I always bought his present last minute—depending on what hint I could glean from him. I remembered our first Christmas—years, and years ago. I was working as an insurance secretary (before I became an agent), and money was scarce. I typed a little book of poems I had written about our romance. And I gave him inexpensive presents I knew he would like—added up to much affection and little money. And he gave me a radio. He was quick to point out it was a Panasonic. I still have that radio. I think his main purpose in giving it was I had such a lousy radio that he hated listening to it. And the years went on when he just "forgot" to get me a present, but even then I always remembered him. Then we went through another phase—where I gave him very expensive gifts and he also gave me nice gifts. And this year—I had no desire to buy him a gift. What was wrong with me? I had always loved getting him presents. But, I knew—I knew—I would not buy him a gift. He would ask me for a hint or a list of what I wanted, and I would simply say it wasn't necessary—that we were not exchanging this year. And I knew he would protest (but be relieved), and he would not just go out and buy one anyhow. No, I knew that would not happen. And I knew, I too, was relieved.

My oldest son would be down from New York State, and I looked forward to his holiday visit. I decorated the house during several successive nights. I have an artificial rather leafless tree near the TV. I leave white lights on it, and decorate it for each season. Now I added an animated Victorian doll at its base and white and gold decorations to its branches. An oriental vase of enormous red flowers rests on a buffet near the front window. I added miniature twinkling colored lights to it. Outside I found a bare branch and spray-painted it a golden hue; placed it in an earthen umbrella stand and decorated it with Victorian bows of purple, and red velvet apples. It twinkled in splendor. In the dining room, a tall floor candlelabra gleamed with miniature white lights. In fact every room in the house would have some evidence of the holidays. I loved doing all this and the little get-together with friends.

<u>But Cassadaga was ever present in my thoughts</u>. I had asked the Rev. Ben for a few lessons on natural laws. There are thousands of God's natural laws that rule our universe. I think this will be a life long study for me. I will give you a study of two, and you will realize what I mean by a "life-long" study.

"<u>The Law of Attraction</u>. There is a magnetic force within ourselves, there are around ourselves a universe and also within ourselves. There is a oneness between yourself and the entire universe. Only time is needed to unfold.

"Magnetic forces travel into the body through the force of interest or desires. Don't let desires control yourself, but learn to control them. We are the sum total of attractions. We can be attracted by all our emotions. There is a certain force to attraction. Annoyances cling to us and are difficult to eliminate because they are attracted to us. We will have to learn the law of elimination of those things that are detrimental to us.

"The magnetic field or forces are established from the chemical kingdom on up through the animal kingdom. It, of course, can be through the emotions or even from the groups of people who get together. This field...what creates attraction? It deals with the law of gravity. We change. We outgrow them. What takes place? What is the essence? It can be based upon desire or needs within ourselves."

O.K., I thought, take a look at this. There are forces at work that draw things to us, forces <u>in</u> us that draw things to us. But our desires, our emotions have much to do with these attractions. We can draw annoyances to us or we can draw good things to us. And it was at this point I thought of Don Zanghi and what strange power of attraction was at work here.

"The force that builds attraction is a need or emptiness within ourselves. We may change or outgrow our attractions. Perhaps something is fulfilled or the need is changed. Two people brought together through the law of attraction was shared anticipation or something. If the other person does not keep pace with us, there is an emptiness, and we change. An attraction may be created by curiosity or wanting to know another. Sometimes sharing of mutual interests makes us grow closer together.

"We should be able to stand aside and look objectively and see if our associations are good for us or bad. Our personality is not only our own but we also take to ourselves those of the persons we are associating with."

And I smiled to myself as I thought of my Grandma saying that one rotten apple can spoil the whole barrel. How our lives would be on a different plane if we made these periodic checks to decide if a person was not a desirable associate, and have the courage to disassociate ourselves before we took on some of those "rotten apple" characteristics!

"It is very necessary to ascertain and observe what we want to have built into our personality. When we identify too closely with a person on a lower level, we take on their characteristics. Only with a spiritual background can we pull out of a bad association. The law operates two ways. We can also associate with those on a higher level, and it will raise us up to a better level."

"Friendship ties-what is the power? It is stimulating attraction. During attraction we put our best foot forward. If it is more than a body attraction, we will gain something beneficial from it. Through the law of attraction, whenever there is a heart-felt interest, either in mental or spiritual plane, when the mind is animated, the mind is stimulated. We grow moment to moment and change."

"We have cycles beginning at the age of five. This is when we are first beginning to think and develop personalities or go on and be able to express ourselves. We have a limited capacity emotionally and spiritually. These cycles run in cycles of seven. From age 12-19 we go through another. We do not reach maturity until we touch 40. Then we develop and unfold, then expand and fold out. At each of these phases, ages 26,33, and 40 we comprehend and then deal with changes in our attraction. Our attractions can be come more spiritual. Earlier we may be under habit patterns or we may have obligations."

I remember my very early religion—Catholicism. I was introduced at an early age (3) and never questioned what I was taught. As a teen religion became more important to me. I recall going to church by myself to pray about test finals at school. Then there was marriage and the obligations and I didn't really get into a spiritual mode again until my late thirties.

"We not only give to others, we also gain from others. Our attractions may have been different, but we have gotten together through a common need, a thing that creates a vacuum draws us. We all have the same need. We can be brought into the spiritual cycle through a loss…someone outgrowing us or we outgrow someone else through the death or loss of someone. There is something in the very forces of life itself that causes us to reach out for that spark of survival. It will seek and reach out for attractions or friendship or even love again to fulfill itself.

"What takes place during a friendship? Our mind is almost present with them. We have established a field of communication. Many times when away from a person, we feel drawn to them and we do not feel the same way when we are with them. We are picking up the loneliness of the other person, and the thought is not our own. We are tuning into another person's thoughts almost continually when we are not projecting thought. Our minds are many times in touch."

How many times have I answered a phone and <u>knew</u> who was calling? Countless times. How often have I thought of a person for days and then finally trekked to the mailbox and found a letter from them. How many times have my sister and I said the same sentence simultaneously? And how many times have you had the same thoughts as a lover? Yes, yes, yes, when you are in tune, you are in tune!

"Attractions can be emotional, spiritual, or mental. Many times during loneliness, there can be a line of attraction during a time of need or necessity. We have a need for nourishment mentally. We seek new interests because we get tired or bored. We will reach out to seek new attractions to answer some need.

We have within ourselves a need to grow and expand. We can get into a state of stagnation unless we get into something new. There is a need to reach out and refresh"

I thought of how bored I was with my life before I journeyed to Cassadaga. Everything was the same old thing. Each day seemed to be a duplicate of the prior day with the same patterns and the same people. I needed—there was a vacuum—and then there was Cassadaga drawn into my life like the tide is drawn by the moon.

"Out of your attraction, how many times has it created an ideal that you want to live up to and the other person's idealization. They aspire to be equal to you. Aspiration can cause us to improve and get better. This is a step of growth. We become charged. We get a new force.

Some people's personalities do this to us. They can charge us on the spiritual plane and also on the mental plane.

"When there is some attraction, look at the change, the transforming power it has on the person. Sometimes people can give you new thoughts. See what it does to you on the mental plane. We are looking for someone who is interested in us as well as someone to be interested in. We have to give in order to receive. This is the power of communication. This is how attractions are cemented. Look at the people who have played a part in your life in the past. How much are you really aware of what the attraction did to you? Think how the attraction made you grow. It depends on what you gained or what negative attitude you developed that might be the seed of the next cycle. Look to the point of the growth and not the negative. Look at the spiritual growth. What you lose on the physical plane, you gain on the spiritual plane. Nothing is lost. It only changes form. Growth is still there and you have gained spiritually.

"You can tend to not want to enter the stream of life again after you have been hurt. You cannot go through grief or loss without finding a certain sense of sensitivity within yourself. Do you want it to be pettiness? Reject self-pity. You will not benefit from the part it plays in your life. But you can take it and by being cheerful, you can make a growth in your soul.

Long forgotten people popped into my mind. I worked on a weekly newspaper in a small town. I wrote a column called the Woman's Angle. The editor, Bob H. gave me carte blanche to write whatever I fancied: book reviews, interviews, personal experiences, etc. He was a totally brilliant man, graduated from some Ivy League college—and at the time I simply had my high school diploma. But, he had read my publicity blurbs for the P.T.A. (No not Harper Valley), and told me I had talent and suggested the column. But he had a problem—the bottle and, in retrospect, a negativism problem (he was an intellectual but wound up running a small town newspaper).

I can still see him sitting behind that editorial desk: a bit rotund, tall, a shock of wonderful white hair, good features, but a tongue that could excoriate a saint. If he disapproved of a sentence or paragraph (and God forbid if it was the whole piece) great gobs of sarcasm would roll from his tongue. He would raise an eyebrow, hunch his shoulders, screw up his mouth and read your ignominious effort. Then read it again and fix an unrelenting eye on you and say "Is that what you really <u>meant</u> to say?" How many times did I walk across the field towards home with tears coursing down my face? But if he was in a really good mood he would heap on the accolades and treat you to lunch.

Did I grow from that relationship? Oh, yes, yes, yes in spite of the hurt. I admired his brilliance. He inspired me to go back to school…and I became an English teacher.

I went back to the notes…"Pain is our growth, and out of that comes a deeper sensitivity. You cannot lose. You increase your sensitivity. When you miss something on the physical plane, you will gain on the spiritual plane.

"People are attracted to us by our need. When you need a thing, you are sincere, stable, eager. Desire can be a momentary thing. Many times we want something and after we get it, we don't want it. But when we <u>need</u> something, we create a vacuum and attract. You attract people who have passed on to another plane after death as you have need. They do not come to us for no reason whatever. They are attracted to you by your aspirations. If you want knowledge, you will attract those who can give you knowledge. If you need healing, you will attract those who can give you healing, not only the ones in the other plane, but those who are also in the living. When you use your ESP, you will have a spiritual teacher or many of them. As we advance and grow, every grade you pass you have another teacher. There are many and new changes as you change. According to the need within yourself, you will have a change of forces.

I remembered my reading with Helene. She told of the needs I would have. If and when I needed a "procedure" for my heart, my

Uncle Ernie would be there helping from the spirit world. And my father was there in the wings ready to help and pave the way in any career I might have in the world of writing. And on <u>this</u> side there was Donald Zanghi who helped with a healing, and the mediums who gave me the advice I needed.

The Law of Attraction worked, it was God's law. From the Rev. Ben's notes I next delved into the Law of Cause and Effect. "First, we want to think in terms of laws of the mind. There are three different attributes that deal with our mind: objective, subjective, and sub-conscious. These are unfolded through interest and enthusiasm. The subjective deals with the immediate things, the things you are dealing with at the present time. We need the ability to analyze these things you are picking up. The subjective is the conscious mind at this moment.

"All the things that have taken place in the past, all opinions, whether based upon truth or falsity, are part of the subconscious. We pass through trials because we believe we are on the path of truth; but when we find out differently, we change. We should realize the power of thought. Back of every action that is preceded by a motive, there is thought. An effect will be produced by the motive. We have a tendency to think about ourselves. We look at ourselves from a favorable standpoint. We don't understand when we are having an ulterior motive.

"Out of everything that is done, the law of compensation is dependent upon motive. We should understand our own motives. Let's say you give a gift. Look at the motive. Was it given with out condition or because of an appeasement or to leave a favorable impression? We can perform a thing without condition, but let us first look at the heart. 'As a man thinketh, so is he'. Out from the heart comes all the issues of life. The heart is kept in perfect action because of the rhythm. This is not only physical. The heart plays a part. The attitude and spirit with which we perform a thing is what counts."

A few months ago I had an interruption. The boy next door asked if he could use my telephone. He is about ten, chunky, a whinny-type of kid. No, I can't say I'm enthusiastic about this boy. And he was interrupting my work. But I let him use the phone. He had obviously skipped school and was calling his Mom. He pleaded with her for a ride to her house. She must have realized he was skipping school (the sore lip excuse just didn't have the ring of truth), and refused to come to his rescue. He left dejectedly.

I should have felt empathy. I had allowed him to use my phone. Was my motive pure? I didn't <u>want</u> him to interrupt to use my phone. Then why had I said yes? I just didn't want <u>him</u> to think I was an unkind person—and <u>I</u> didn't want to think of my-self as an unkind person. My <u>attitude</u> left a lot to be desired, and I'm sure that in the akashic record I did not get Brownie points.

"Every action has some reaction. That is a manifestation of life. The things that we do unconditionally are free...free gift or action. It can be a word of encouragement. When given with sincerity, there is bound to be a constructive benefit. It will come back to you. Cause and effect."

And again I thought of the boy phone caller. He had come home from school with a "hurt lip", just to spend a day with his Mom. He wanted to play—not work. His action did get a reaction, but not the one he desired. Instead of spending the day playing at Mom's he had to spend the remainder of the day at his Dad's home...alone.

"Out of every thought and action following a thought there is always something that comes back to us. If we expect no compensation, we are not limiting that power. It is like keeping an open door between yourself and the spiritual world. That takes place on the spiritual level of your being. The things that we do and the good that comes never comes back from the one you did it to. Your good comes from the universal force, not from the recipient. That which comes from the recipient is limited.

"If you are going to do a thing by just trying to appease a situation, there is a certain limitation in the effect that is produced. Something is not worked out because you have not thought out the motivation. There is still some karmic debt somewhere down the line. Understand your motive and face your weakness. Have the ability to admit your mistakes and errors. If you are not in truth with yourself, you are divided. That split in yourself is like an alibi and keeps you from the oneness of God. Our own attitudes are what cause the partition. We cannot touch the universal until we understand our motives. If there is a certain condition that is connected with whatever we do and that is some personal motivation, the power of the spirit is restricted."

And I thought of <u>myself</u> and so <u>many</u> of the people I know who justify-justify-justify. And they wind up lying to <u>themselves</u>.

"How many times we are under certain habit patterns, that is personality patterns. We act the same way under emotional stress or when we get angry. These can be altered and changed through knowledge and understanding. When we comprehend and see the working of our own mind and what we are doing to ourselves, we can alter and change and make our minds more receptive and increase our powers of awareness. Analyze and see if what you do is a habit pattern. If it is not in your heart, there is a spirit of reluctance. Unless you can do something wholeheartedly, you should give it a second thought before you promise to do something."

Can you really look at your emotional patterns face—to face? I have one relative who takes umbrage at the most meaningless innuendo—who turns, glares—and gives a snide remark regardless if the remark was said in innocence. This happens all the time. I have another relative that was so jealous of her husband (who was elderly and not attractive) she would not let him out of her sight. Every woman (even her daughter) was a threat. And she reacted with wrath towards the husband and the woman she suspected. This happened constantly—a habit. And I, when hurt or filled with negative emotion, tend to clam up and run away from the situation. I would be better off to confront the situation, talk it out, and forget it. But I cover my emotions and run off to lick my wounds. Habit, habit—that <u>CAN</u> be changed.

"It is not always the act of commission but the act of omission, that means we suffer a karmic debt—through some act that we didn't do. This will leave an emptiness because we were not sincere. When we speak of cause, it is the invisible, and <u>effect</u> is what is made manifest. It originates from that which is not tangible. It may not have been just the day before but it may have been years in the past. We should try to keep our life in balance so that we are neither reaping karmic results or creating new karma. The thought is the seed of what will be produced later on. All things work in a cycle. When we can stand in the other person's shoes, if we create an error of omission, there will be something that we will be deprived of. Life in the invisible realm balances things. It is through this that we gain understanding.

I remembered all the times I wanted to speak a word of encouragement to someone, but didn't have the "nerve", all the times I passed someone who needed a ride, and didn't quite dare, all the times I should have given of my time or my finances—and didn't. Now that kind of incident left me with guilt—and I'm sure—Karmic debt.

"It is very important to live in the moment you are in. Don't worry about the future or you are creating worry which is a negative condition. If you go into the past, you cannot change it. Stay in the time of the <u>now</u>. What you have a tendency to worry about will melt away.

I think this is a hard lesson. If we are experiencing great joy—it is easy to live in the <u>now</u>. But if we are in pain or in boredom—we want to escape to the future or the past. I just had a kitty put to sleep (cancer) and I tend to want to relive all his past moments. I know I must let those thoughts go and get on with the now moment—but it is difficult.

"Observe your motive and cause. We have been through grief and loss, distress, loneliness, trials, etc. which give us a good compassion. It is understanding, the ability to see yourself and where you are, the things that upset you. It is out of that comprehension that makes you able to help."

"Here is the most important thing when we pray. We continue to pray over and over and over. That thing has not left your consciousness to be productive. You hold on to what you ask for. You never release it. It is like planting a seed and continually digging it up to see if it has grown. We do not pray correctly. We should not pray over and over again for the same thing. Are we afraid that God is not going to answer? Faith is the ability to let loose of a thing, not hang on to it. Universal mind cannot take over until we let loose of it. This is true of many of the problems we face from day to day. Release them and let go."

Just think about it—when we ask God for a thing over and over—we are really worrying—not having faith that God will handle it. <u>Asking once is enough</u>. Turn it over to God and forget it. I have an old car I have been trying to sell. I have placed it in God's hands, but have I really? Every time I see it I wonder why it hasn't sold. When I think of it—it is with apprehension—not faith that the sale is already accomplished—in God's time. And I know the only way it will sell, is my just forgetting it—realizing it truly is no more my concern, but now lies in higher hands.

"Think in terms of what you want, you hold it from you because you see it apart from you. You do not see it as part of you. You keep distance between yourself and it. Think in terms of possessing it and you will quickly receive it. Whether it is a talent, accomplishment, or something to be fulfilled, this is the way to get it. Don't separate yourself from that which you want. Don't see it apart and wish for something or you create a distance between yourself and it. Say, I am a thing, or I have a thing, and see yourself with it. Don't observe it at a distance. Enter into a thing and become that thing, and feel it. Identify with what you want and you have it. But you can't identify with a thing if you project into tomorrow or sometime in the future. Don't separate yourself from the very thing you are striving for.

I thought of my son and his engineering corporation. He was still struggling with it after six years. He "wanted" it to be financially successful. The more he dwelled on the "want," the less business he seemed to have. He was taking a paycheck about once a month. Things looked bleak. Finally, one morning at about six o'clock I was inspired to call him. I'm not a Mom who gives advice, but this felt inspirational. I told him that little secret—that if he asked God simply "wanting" success—he would always be "wanting." But if he thanked God for the success he would soon bring him—things would turn around. However, he had to sincerely believe the success was there waiting for him. He had to have faith—claim the success. I told him that was exactly why everything his younger brother did (whatever venture) was successful. I did not hear from Winston for about three weeks, but when I did, he said the marketing person had lined up a few jobs. And a month ago they landed a fat contract. I think he listened to Mom.

"It is easy for us to enter into a negative thing. How many times do we think of things from a positive standpoint? This requires building. This requires effort. This takes energy. Would you have developed the same personality if you had been brought up in a different environment? You are in this body for a reason, and you have a thing to fulfill. If you do not have a place to use your talent, of what benefit is it to you? Like the law of supply and demand. The demand increases as the supply decreases. And we find the same with our talents. Our talents would be of no use without humanity. Work, sharing or utilizing your talent in some way is your reason for being here. Look and evaluate things and know whether there will be fullness out of what you have done or your motive in carrying out your reaction."

I thought of my boredom of a few months ago. And I thought of my guilt because I <u>wasn't</u> writing. Yes, I think we feel a sin of omission when we just waste our talents. We are to share what we have been given. I remembered the poem I wrote after my ex-husband's death. The poem was inspired by my feelings about his death, and the poem helped me resolve those feelings. But I didn't feel fulfilled until the poem was read at his funeral, until the poem was published in several newspapers, until the poem was published in an anthology. Why?

For ego? No, because "our talents would be of no use without humanity." Those who read the poem could relate to my feelings of lose, and perhaps could be helped from some feelings with which they were burdened. If I write, and the article or book sits on a shelf—I have only helped myself and not others. Then there is guilt again. The most difficult part is getting your work into print. I recall one of the happiest work periods of my life was in writing the weekly column for the local newspaper. I felt so alive and so fulfilled. Yes, I was married and was raising my three sons and that, too, was a purpose for my life. But, at the same time, using my writing talent gave me enormous joy and satisfaction. I felt God was in the world and in my heart and all was right.

"Don't do anything with a condition. With this spirit, there is a limit and restriction. You have placed a limitation on it. It can only move in a certain capacity. You limit your unfoldment. 'Take ye no thought of self. He who seeks to save his life shall lose it.' The same is true with motivation and causes. If you are seeking whatever it is from a standpoint of trying to preserve it for yourself, you limit its power of activity later. If you can lose yourself in the interest on the soul plane of yourself, blend in consciousness with yourself; you will seek the interest of your area all around you and see from the realm of the invisible and shape up in the affairs around you and expand the range of consciousness.

"Think back when you did something with no thought of reward. See if you can do something with complete un-selfishness. Even things done for your loved ones are through selfishness because they belong to you and you don't want to lose them.

"You can determine whether a thing will be fruitful or not by your attitude, whether it is sincere or not. There are opportunities. Everything travels on a circuit. You are in touch with universal spirit if you have the attitude of love when you perform a thing. Whatever you do will come back to you. 'Cast your bread upon the waters and after many days it will come back to you.'"

My thanks to the Rev. Ben for his two studies on The Law of Attraction and the Law of Cause and Effect. There are thousands of natural or universal laws set up by God. And to be in harmony with God's laws—just might be a life-long study.

7

Spiritualism: Philosophy, Science, Religion

As I left for Colby I viewed my house with delight—Christmas had infiltrated everything. And my son from upper New York State would soon be here. I pulled out of the driveway with Mag, "1 feel about to burst with Christmas spirit," I exclaimed. "The house decorations are great," Mag observed as we headed for Cassadaga.

After the service we went for refreshments. Don was already at the table talking to another medium. "Oh, I've had a past life in Egypt," he countered. My ears perked up. I know some mediums, including Don, did believe in reincarnation.

"You do past life regressions, don't you?" I asked. He handed me his business card and I read: past life and regressive therapy, massage therapy, clinical hypnosis, lectures, and UFO Alien abduction research. Well, I thought, a renaissance man, indeed.

"Maybe if I got regressed I'd discover the reason why I seem to be going in circles without getting anywhere, why I can't seem to settle for the right job, or return to school or whatever." Mag said.

"I should have a thing about heights, since I fell off a mountain in Peru in a past incarnation," Don laughed.

"Well, I have observed you may be a 'little' klutsy, but how the heck did you fall off a mountain?" I asked.

"Oh, you guys know how I am—talking, talking. I had a group of students with me, and I was explaining something, and I turned to face them, gesturing with my hands, and I felt my left foot slip, then felt myself falling off the mountain, The Mountain of the Moon.

"And I presume that was the end of that lifetime," Mag laughed.

I thought of my dolls—why was I so possessed about collecting dolls? Perhaps the answer was in a past life. And what about the men I was attracted to—I made sure they were quite unobtainable. So many recurrent patterns in my life—and I'm sure there had to be karmic reasons for it all.

"Don, do you think I would be a worthy subject for this regression and hypnosis? I mean I'm not sure I could be hypnotized. But, I think maybe my present would be less confusing if I knew something of my past lives."

"That's the main reason for doing it," he replied, to help the situation in the now."

As I arose to leave I told him, "Let me ponder this, it may be something I want to do." I knew it would have to be at his office in Deland. The Spiritualists at the camp did not approve of hypnotism being used on the grounds, so Don's office was used for his other business activities.

At the camp, I began another study—the study of spiritualism: (the definition,) as a philosophy, as a science, and as a religion.

I went to a class taught by the Rev. Phil Allen who discussed the actual definition of Spiritualism, and its history. "Before the rise of the Western world, science, philosophy and religion were not really separated. Religion (under the Christians) separated the three. Medicine further separated them. Many well-known people such as Gov. Talmadge were in spiritualistic study during the 1800s. But fraud got into the practice of spiritualism, and the ensuing publicity caused the governor to resign his post.

As a result mental mediumship rather than physical phenomena was advocated. Prior to this, Congress had even appropriated $60,000 for the study of Spiritualism. Science is the 'how' of things: we discern by the facts. If our lives are God-inspired we observe our progress in life.

Mediumship proves things and healing allows communication and observation. As a philosophy Spiritualism is based. on love, not fear or guilt. People develop through love-based, not fear-based philosophy. As a religion, we have conscious union with the divine. Our religion is demonstrated through the Golden Rule where we put someone else's interest over our own."

I now turn to a handout given to us by Rev. Allen. Many of his notes were based on: THE QUESTIONNAIRE and PROPHETS, SEERS and RELIGIONS by Peggy Barnes, N.S.A.C. Spiritualist MANUAL, LECTURE NOTES TO THE SCHOOL OF WISDOM by Geoffrey Hodson, THE ROCK OF TRUTH by Arthur Findlay.

"Briefly: Spiritualism is the Science, Philosophy, and Religion of CONTINUOUS LIFE, based upon the demonstrated fact of communication, by means of mediumship, with those who LIVE in the Spirit World. The key phrase here is CONTINUOUS LIFE. We do not believe that the chain is ever broken between life and death, and for lack of a better word, resurrection. In the blink of an eye, we arrive in the Spirit World with all our loved ones we knew here and some we only know on the other side. Our personality survives and we are basically the same there as we were here. We don't suddenly sprout wings or lay sleeping until judgment day. All of this is proven by mediumship through communication with those gone on before us.

"WHAT SPIRITUALISM IS AND DOES: It teaches personal responsibility. It removes all fear of death, which is really the portal of the spirit world. It teaches that death is not the cessation of life, but a mere change of condition. It teaches, not that a man has a soul, but that man is a soul and has a body. That man is a spiritual being now, even while encased in flesh. That as a man sows on earth he reaps in the life to come. That those who have passed on are conscious—not asleep. That communication between the living and the 'dead' is scientifically proven, by mediumship and observation. It thus brings comfort to the bereaved, and alleviates sorrow. It brings to the surface man's spiritual gifts, such as inspiration, clairvoyance, clairaudiance, and healing powers. It teaches that the spark of divinity dwells in all. That as a flower gradually unfolds in beauty, so does the spirit of man unfold and develop in the spirit spheres. Spiritualism is God's message to mortals declaring that THERE IS NO DEATH. That all who have passed on still live. That there is hope in the life beyond for the most sinful. That EVERY soul will progress through the ages to heights, sublime and glorious, where God is LOVE and LOVE is God. It is a manifestation, a demonstration and a proof of the continuity of life and of the many Spirit manifestations recorded in the Christian Bible. It demonstrates the many spiritual gifts with which mankind is endowed but which through want of knowledge have been allowed to lie dormant, or through prejudice have been violently and unjustly suppressed. Personal liberty is always encouraged and should <u>never</u> be suppressed in anyone's name or cause."

In my reading with medium Helene L. I was amazed at how much the spirits were true to their personality on <u>this</u> <u>side</u>. My ex—husband was <u>always</u> concerned with money and security. Our biggest marital discords were over finances. And his message to me had been to be careful—budget the money—don't overspend. My Dad who was a sweetie, very kind, was concerned with Mom's health, and was quick to reassure me her death or passing would not entail a nursing home (and I am sure he wanted me to pass this on to her). Uncle Ernie was a giving person who idolized his wife. His message to her was simply one of profound gratitude. Yes, their personalities were very much intact on the Spirit side of life.

"The most profound feeling by most who come to understand Spiritualism and believe is the fact that they lose their fear of death. "Spiritualism is a science because it investigates, analyzes and classifies facts and manifestations demonstrated from the spirit side of life. Spiritualism is a religion. Because it studies the laws of nature both on the seen and the unseen sides of life and bases its conclusions upon present and observed facts. It accepts statements of observed facts of past ages and conclusions drawn there from, when sustained by reason, and by results of observed facts of present day. Spiritualism is a religion because it strives to understand and to comply with the physical, mental and spiritual laws of nature, which are the laws of God."

And now comes the sticky burr that will cause much consternation when viewed by my orthodox Christian mother and younger son. I have already had multitudinous discussions with them about the Bible and Jesus. They believe every word (even the contradictions) are to be taken literally—I don't.

"Two commonly asked questions will be briefly discussed that are generally asked by newcomers in the western hemisphere. They are:

1.   Do Spiritualists believe in the Bible?

2.   Do you believe in Jesus?"

"Of course we believe in the Bible. We believe it to be the religious guide of this Christian era. Spiritualism is based upon the Bible and if all the Spiritualism were taken from it there would be little left but history. We know that its many books were written by different men and these men, while writing inspirationally, were bound to insert more or less of their own personal beliefs.

"The Bible has been translated many, many times and each time there have been changes in the wording. Therefore we, as Spiritualists, do not believe the Bible to be the absolute word of God. God did not give man all there was to know about religion at the time the Bible was written, for man was not ready to receive it. Religion has evolved down through the centuries just as all other things have, and a man can only grasp it little by little as he progresses. He has a long way to travel yet before he can understand and apply to his individual life and conduct the actual teachings of the Sermon on the Mount.

"Spiritualism also recognizes the fact that the Christian Bible is not the only Bible containing truth. There is truth in all bibles and the fundamentals governing good behavior are the same whether they be derived from the Vedas, the Avesta, the Koran, or the New Testament.

"Spiritualists have a practical understanding of Jesus and of his teachings. They recognize the man, Jesus, as the greatest teacher and medium of our age. A man who demonstrated for three short years a religion that has survived for centuries had a real message for mankind. As a God of miraculous birth we do not worship him but as a son of God, our elder brother and one of the greatest prophets of all time, we kneel at his feet in admiration for his wonderful demonstration of right living. We recognize the fact that he understood the Natural Law of God better than any man who has ever lived and without doubt was sent by Divine Mind with an inspired message to mankind; that glorious manifestation that proved for all time the continuity of life and the return of Spirit."

And thus ended the lecture and handout of the Rev. Phil Allen.

Christmas was nearing, and my heart was filled with the Christ spirit—the spirit of doing right and being right with my fellow humans. There is a Christ-spirit through out the season—I felt it as a child and I still feel it. My house now waited for my son, and the dinners, and the gift-giving and the love of all.

Our next lesson was on the philosophy of Spiritualism. The Rev. Sam Nickols led this lecture. "Spiritualist say the <u>self</u> is responsible. We are here to learn. The Golden Rule is vague: You cannot give to another that which he is not prepared to receive or take from another that which he is not prepared to give. There are no mistakes in life—just lessons. There are no coincidences—just lessons. Start understanding the Natural Laws. Think of Karma, of cause and effect. Life is an action that causes a reaction. No two of us will have the identical gift. We must learn to aspire to spiritual enlightenment. We are immortal and will be held accountable for our thoughts and deeds.

"Think of cloning. Identical twins have different personalities. You can't clone the soul. The body is just the envelop. God had a purpose for each soul.

"Don't be afraid to venture into new things. We fear venturing into new ground. The dread or fear is worse than the action. Dread of the dentist is worse than the visit.

"Play each day to the best of your abilities. We need to exercise new pleasures and new truths. We must learn to see the 'whole' picture to understand self. Our attitude is important-we can live with fear or with love. Start each day with the right attitude."

And I did thank God that I was able to overcome my fear of Cassadaga (all the unfounded rumors), and come to Colby and learn of new truths and new pleasures.

I walked into the building with a song in my heart. I knew the next lecturer would be Don Zanghi. He was putting some chairs near a table as I arrived. "Well, don't you look handsome," I observed, noting his light tan jacket and brown trousers.

"And you don't look too shabby yourself," he laughed taking in my lilac jacket and matching wide-brimmed hat. I didn't feel guilty about the compliment—after all—he was a man divorcing. And I knew—I had made the decision—I would have a past-life regression. I would tell him when the opportunity seemed right.

Don began his topic: The Science of Spiritualism:

"Spiritualism is a science because it analyzes, investigates and classifies facts and manifestations from the spirit side of life. Who would think you could meld spirit study with science? Much of mainstream science is still closed off to the phenomena of anything spiritual. Dr. Carl Sagan says, 'Extraordinary claims require extraordinary evidence.' Why? Why does anything but what scientists want to study have to go under different rules and regulations? It comes right down to science needing to accept the experience of the individual. The scientific method is useful in labs, but in spiritual or psychic phenomena the repeatability isn't always on demand. If science can break out of its shell they will realize that the phenomenon of spiritualism is real.

In 1848 the Fox sisters used physical phenomena such as levitation of objects, manifested spirit (right before you), knocks and raps, and trumpet levitation.

"In the beginning, physical phenomena seemed to come first-perhaps to get the attention. It's one thing to give a message to a person and that one person understands it, but it is quite another thing for a group to be sitting around a table (contacting spirit) and the table jumps up and down. That means we all experience it. It grabs attention. Early scientists began to investigate manifestations of spiritualism. They used crude methods such as tying up mediums and putting them in cages in order to disprove fraud. There was no fraud. Then there was the case of DD. Home who demonstrated levitation: he floated out a window, across a street to another building. There wasn't much dispute about that! From that point a number of organizations here and in Britain grew."

I could see Don getting excited—really wound up in his subject. I knew he was approaching something dear to his heart.

"One cannot discount personal experience. For myself, many years ago, I wondered about levitation. I knew if I actually saw it I would be convinced of many things. We had a seance at my home. There were a number of people from the Spiritualist Camp there. We sat around a heavy table. During the seance the table began to move, to wobble up and down, and spin at top speed. Then a trumpet laying on the table floated up in front of my nose and landed in front of another. There were no strings, no wires, the trumpet floated. It was in my house, and I saw it, it was demonstrated scientifically."

"Why is science against this? Science doesn't want to admit the SOUL. Why this separation of spirit and science? DesCartes dabbled in these things. Then the church stepped in and there was a schism. Today church and science are separated. Some scientists as individuals see some light. Here at Cassadaga we had workshops from a professor at Yale and a Harvard professor teaching that went beyond physics.

"Now we hear about 'remote viewing'. This is nothing but the scientific term for clairvoyance. Read <u>The Psychic Warrior</u> by David Morehouse. This deals with the early military experiments with remote viewing: separate departments for channeling, tarot cards etc. The military hides this—but it is the scientific use of clairvoyance.

"Today we have spirit communication through electronic means. There is communication through radio, tapes, and TV. It is two-way communication from the spirit world. It is science in practice—using modern methods instead of the 'trumpet of old'.

Don gave us his famous smile and as he sat down I wondered what the spirits could tell me about him—why I felt that I had always known him.

At home my Christmas goodies were in the freezer and I was making plans for the big dinner. I loved planning the many dishes and getting much in readiness the week prior. My son would arrive within the week. I enjoyed spending time with him. We both loved the Daytona flee market and I knew we would be there picking up last minute Christmas gifts and his presents for co—workers and friends.

We had one more lecture before the holidays. The Rev. Raymond A. Burton would lecture on the Religion of Spiritualism. The Rev. Raymond began the talk, but it became a group thing as one after another started voicing opinions. The group discussion went as follows: "There are truths in all religious texts. Spiritualists believe in personal responsibility. This is not a religion based on fear. Don't read just one Bible, read all Bibles.

"We cut across the basis of all religions. The study and the proving means we can question. We each have our own path. Christianity follows someone's dogma. We do as Jesus did—we heal, we have individual growth. We are ready to serve.

"We are Masters in embryo—we could be like Jesus. We have responsibility: obey natural law. We pay for our own deeds and actions. Jesus probably wouldn't recognize His church today.

"The Bible really wasn't stared until 350 years after Christ was dead. The Council at Constantine really rewrote it…they took out reincarnation.

"We must know God is part of us. God is within. We are all connected. You must respect all as part of God. Jesus said, 'Know you not that you are Gods?' Don't look upward to God. UNDERLINE{LOOK WITHIN."

From the Rev. Raymond A. Burton's handout: "SPIRITUALISM:

The view that spirit is a prime element of reality. A belief that spirits (of the dead) communicate with the living through a medium. It is a movement comprising religious organizations emphasizing spiritualism. RELIGION: the service of worship of God or the supernatural; commitment or devotion to a religion faith or observance; a personal set or institutionalized system of religious attitudes beliefs or practices. A cause, a principle or set of principles, or a system of beliefs held to with ardor and faith.

"A set of Principles: We have nine that we strive to live by. You often hear in our church that we are not a dogmatic religion, and we aren't. You also will hear that we have no creed. I believe that statement is an attempt to emphasize to others our belief in personal responsibility and free will and choice.

"Creed: A brief authoritative formula of religious beliefs or principles. Not only do we have a creed, but we may have one of the strongest creeds of all religions. The nine principles we have adopted constitute our creed. I do not believe that you can have a true religion without a creed."

The handout elaborates, "This is not a 'take it on faith my son/daughter' type of religion. I cannot tell you how many times, when I was studying for the Ministry, and I questioned the dogma, I was told, 'Take it on faith'. That is something that we as Spiritualists do not have to do. We as Spiritualist recognize that here are truths in all religious tests, as well as the truths passed on to us from mystics throughout the ages. But it does not stop there, we are encouraged to speak to God in prayer and to listen to God/Spirit through meditation, mediumship, mysticism, dreams and other means, accept the truths that resonate within us, and hold to these truths as our own.

"Some of the main differences between Spiritualism and other religions is that we do not proselytize, that we teach Personal Responsibility, Free Will and Choice; that personal responsibility is put to work in our daily lives with the Divine guidance, the Higher Teachings that we receive through our communication with spirit.

"We hold to that truth that we are all part of that one main source. Part of one great soul, a spark of God, and therefore through personal choice, free will, with personal responsibility and divine guidance through communication with spirit, we are co—creators with that Infinite Source—God.

"We know that the Religion of Spiritualists, is based on the continuity of life; that God's promise of eternal life is true, as proven through the phenomena of Spiritualism; that we each have personal responsibility, and must obey nature's physical and spiritual laws, what we sometimes call natural law, which is the formula given to us to live a perfect life in harmony and balance with this perfect universe.

"Spiritualism is a True Religion!"

And so ended the final lesson before Christmas. Mag and I went to the Grove for refreshments. And as always I was some how drawn to Don's table.

"And how is life—how is actually <u>living</u> in Cassadaga?" I queried.

He took a sip of coffee and replied, "I love it here," but he looked a little sad.

"And are you ready for Christmas, bought all the gifts, etc.?" I asked. He had lived with his wife and the children last year. He must be feeling lonely.

"I guess Christmas will be a little lean" he said without the usual Zanghi smile.

All the people were chit-chatting and enjoying their refreshments. My heart skipped a beat. What could I do to make his Christmas better? I thought of the past-life regression I planned to have in January. Oh, how obtuse—I could pay him in advance!

"If a person were to have an office visit in January—would it be possible for that person to make the payment—in advance. Depending, of course, if it didn't cost an arm and leg? Like how much is an office visit?"

He pulled out one of his cards, wrote a figure on it and said, If that is too much you might want to break it into two payments."

Mag was talking to the lady opposite. I looked at the card and smiled, "I don't think this is a problem, Don," I said. I started to pull out my checkbook.

"Are you sure you want to do this before the appointment?" he asked. I could see he felt awkward. I put my hand on his arm to reassure him.

"So I'm paying in advance for a January appointment, and at the same time making the holiday a little easier for you makes me happy," I assured him.

He took the check, and followed Mag and I to the door.

"You can't stay longer?"

"Sorry, dinner with Mom. But have a wonderful Christmas," He hugged us good-bye and Mag and I left. Somehow I knew this day, and this event, had glorified my whole Christmas.

8

Lyceums

And Christmas arrived: the house was redolent with roasting turkey; the table glittered with brass charger plates and golden flatware. I was pleased, and ready for my guests. Son Winston, had arrived and we had done the flee markets and enjoyed our "cup of Christmas tea." Out of the blue—I thought of Don and hoped he was having these special moments too.

As good times do, the holidays passed all too quickly, and I knew I was ready to resume my lessons at Cassadaga.

Our first subject was the <u>SOUL</u>, led by Theresa Hamilton. She told us the soul is the real self that goes on learning and becomes more refined; it is the crown and glory of cosmic life; it is immortal in nature; the mind is the thinking part of soul; soul tone has specific vibrations; there is a higher mental body. In the discussion we spoke of the soul as light reaching to a higher realm; the soul as a connection between us and God; of spiritual growth causing the soul to grow; that the soul really knows all—that we just have to 'remember'; the soul works its way back up with mind and spirit helping it along; mind is a function of spirit and that the soul is here because it wants it's earthly experience.

I like January in Florida: I like the mild, balmy 80 degree days sans the humidity, and I like the sudden influx of cold from the North—the 30 degree days where hands feel frozen and you run to the sweater closet. Zippy, I just love it.

Our next lecturer was Dr. Harold Warren. I always look forward to hearing from this elegant, eloquent gentleman. His topic was <u>mental</u>

mediumship. He spoke in detail on the many types of mental mediumship. "Chairvoyance is clear seeing. If objective it is caused through a link with the pineal gland and if subjective you see with the eye (see spirit around a person). The spiritualist will see the spirit entity as real as he sees a living person. Eighty percent of clairvoyance is the subjective.

"There is a major difference between being a psychic and being a medium. All of us have the more basic psychic ability. It can be done without a spirit teacher. Mediums, however, are on a finer level. There are many fine psychics but they do not pick up on spiritual entities. Mediums have both abilities.

"Clairaudience is clear hearing. In the subjective the spirit voice appears to be in the inner ear or head. In the objective you hear spirit outside the ear—just like a person talking.

"Exray Clairvoyance happens when one can see through solid objects. It was formerly known as transparency. One can practice this in meditation.

"Traveling clairvoyance is when you can leave your body and travel—to the earthplane or spirit world. The more modern term for, this is remote viewing.

"Auric clairvoyance is psychic in nature. It is also electromagnetic in nature. You see the energy or colors around a person. You may see a mist of clear colors, and they fluctuate with a person's thoughts. The colors may reflect different meanings—even about the person's health.

"Trance clairvoyance means the medium enters a state of trance. The message is given during the trance; even the medium doesn't know what is happening. The messages are not usually any better than a regular reading.

"Clairscenscience deals with the feelings, intuition, solar plexus. You sense something before it happens. You do not disregard your intuition. Intuition will never send you in the wrong direction—it is trying to help you.

"Clairsavoance is clear tasting. Spirit may have liked a certain food, and communicating this—you will know it is that particular person in spirit. A medium may pick up a certain taste like medicine or blood.

"Clairsentience is clear smelling. The medium may clearly smell a rose or some other odor."

When Dr. Warren explained this specific of mental mediumship I thought of my sister and the smell of roses. Her husband gave her roses on special occasions during the marriage. After he passed, she came back from the funeral, opened the door to her house, and was overwhelmed by the scent of roses. This happened on several occasions thereafter. He, from spirit, was clearly trying to tell her he was alive in the spirit world.

"Pschchometry is a kind of soul measurement. The medium gives a reading using an object."

In my case Helene Liberte used a bangle bracelet I wore daily to give her insight.

"Inspirationalism is when great splurges of inspiration come over a person. This just happens. If it occurs when you are writing, just go with it, don't worry about spelling or grammar, just go with your inspiration, Dr. Warren concluded.

I returned home one night, turned on the television to some movie with a desert scene. I watched the sand, palm trees and of a sudden another scene was reeling in my mind.

I could see the picture in my head clearly. A group of horses moved down a sandy road. I could almost feel the heat, the dust, the sweat on the horses. It was a group of soldiers and the metal of their uniforms, the metal of their helmets, shone in the sun. They passed a house and a girl stood watching them pass. The lead soldier turned and stared into the eyes of the girl. I could see the lead soldier. He turned and looked at the girl again. The soldier in that strange uniform was—Donald Zanghi.

I nearly jumped out of my chair. What was I seeing? How could I explain anything so peculiar? The girl was in a long flowing dress. I don't recall anything like the uniforms, even in pictures. The house was of a very thick-wall construction, simple, peasantlike. What a trick of the imagination, I concluded, as I went to the kitchen for a cup of tea to settle my nerves.

And if nerves needed sparking that could have happened at the lecture where The Rev. Sandra Moore spoke on physical mediumship. Sandra spoke about the beginning of modern spiritualism and then she and several others spoke of their <u>experiences</u> with physical phenomena. I had never seen "table tipping" and was quite fascinated by the subject.

She began to talk about the Fox sisters, "Modern spiritualism began in western New York state about 1848. A family with two teen-age daughters moved into a so-called 'haunted' house. There were areas of coldness in the house and they kept hearing 'rappings'. When the girls rapped, the spirits rapped back. Finally the family moved out—but the spirits <u>followed</u> them. The Fox girls were in tune to the spirits and began to give lectures about it. At times they were body searched or even tied up to disclaim any idea of fraud. They had hard lives, but thanks to them the modern movement began.

Sandra explained her experience with spirits and 'table tipping'. The idea is that spirits are asked to come in and answer yes or no questions. How does this happen? Usually a prayer is said to bring the right spirits into the group. Then singing is begun to raise the energy. Spirit probably draws from this energy. Questions are asked and the table (the group touches) levitates and tips to give a yes or no answer. Sandra said, "Perhaps people wouldn't believe this now, but at the table-tipping I attended the table took off and we chased it all over the room. We also heard raps and snapping noises—the noises came from all over the room. Rapping can also get the movement going. On another occasion we were in a restaurant and called in spirit and it began very quickly with table levitation—and we stopped that rather speedily."

A student in the lyceum, Kathy, recalled a two hour experience with table-tipping. The people took turns asking questions, and the energy became highly accelerated with the singing.

Ben Thomas, our assistant minister, and former school principal, told of two experiences. "My sister in spirit, Katherine, spoke to me in two different seances. A trumpet was used as the instrument. The trumpet levitated to yes and no questions. This is confirmation that there is life after death. Spirit exists. I also saw a tambourine jingle in tune to the songs we sang. I attended a session in which spirits left mementos. We placed 3x5 cards in a basket—blank cards. We mediated. When we again looked at the cards, there was the name of the person and a spirit drawn picture on each. And did you know that Abraham Lincoln was a spiritualist? He went to seances, but most people didn't realize he was there. Once, Lincoln sat on a piano and spirit levitated the piano with him seated on it."

Sandra also spoke of the physical phenomena of using photographic paper. At one group blank photographic paper was held to the spiritual chakras (on the back of the person) and the paper didn't turn black as it usually does when exposed to light, it showed colors around the chakras—depicting the energy.

The 'trumpets' spoken of are not musical trumpets, but a funnel-like object about a foot or two long. When spirit is called in, the trumpet levitates to give yes or no answers.

Sandra concluded that she can feel the energy in a town.

She says she feels the energy in Cassadaga is peaceful. Another couple (Joe and Rhonda) said they had visited an Indian burial mound at Blue Springs and felt a tremendous amount of energy at the site.

Don Zanghi was attending the class too. As I looked at him the room seemed to fade away. Again I was watching a scene unfold in my mind. I was <u>viewing</u> the scene, but at times could almost <u>feel</u> the desert heat as the group of horses went down the road; the dust rising from their hooves, the sweat glistening on their rumps. The sun shone brightly on the metal of the armory the helmets gleamed in the brightness. The girl was behind a low enclosure, but very visible from the road that wound directly in front of the adobe-like house. The lead soldier sat straight, with good posture, on his horse. He was muscular and dark. When he turned to look at the girl—there was no mistaking the Donald Zanghi face—the Donald Zanghi eyes—the Donald Zanghi smile.

I mentally pulled myself back into the room. Don looked across at me—and smiled—the very same smile.

Our next lecturer was Gary Edwards, a professor who teaches comparative religion at two colleges. He talked to us about spiritual growth. He told us there was a distinct difference between "religion" and spiritualism. Most religions connect with rituals. Spiritualists are individualistic rather than ritualistic. Growth in spiritualism is concerned with a more simplistic approach with less possessions (shades of Thoreau), with experience equating to knowledge, and with the need for leisure to pursue wisdom (like Whitman and the appreciation of the common things).

He continued, "Sensitivity is a great quality of spirituality. We must be sensitive to (1) self. We must learn to relax the body and get rid of physical stress. We must be sensitive to (2) others like teachers and those around us. We must be sensitive to our environment. We must be sensitive to the spiritual dimension (4), to the spirits around us. They exist there, like the angels and the spirit guides. We must be sensitive to the source of things (5) like the layers of heaven. The soul has come from the source. It animates us. We know the body is left behind, not the soul. Many things change: emotions change, thoughts change, karma keeps coming back. Surrender the thoughts and the karma: the soul is above this. We are part of the divine self."

I needed that lecture, I had a bit of the January 'blahs'. After the excitement of the holidays, there seems to be a general let down in spirit. But, I thought, nothing like the bored spirit I had originally brought with me to Cassadaga. I had been on a long journey of learning and progressing. And I smiled—yes, yes, yes, I had progressed in spirit—I felt that in my heart—and yes in my very soul. One of these days I would apply for membership as a spiritualist at the Southern Camp at Cassadaga.

Our final lecturer was the Rev. Fred Jason who expounded about spirit and the spirit world. "On a daily basis we can get spirit messages. We are spirits wearing garments of flesh. We have a spirit body that keeps our physical body alive. It lasts—survives physical death. This spirit body looks like the physical body with a spiritual brain and all the senses.

"Jesus said 'all I have done, you can do greater'. We must develop our receptivity. Part of this is the healing. Jesus demonstrated this energy.

"Requiring or needing is a resource. If motivation is clear we can access any resource we need.

The spiritual world has a higher vibrational pattern. We must really focus our attention to tune into spirit energy. Spirits can still be pulled by the gravitational pull of the earth."

Fred told us his Aunt was a temporary guide to him for two years. She worked with him temporarily during that time she was needed. Spirits are also evolving and in helping us they are helping themselves too. Be aware of your spirit guides. As we evolve here, we may have different spirit guides. We get whatever help we need.

"On the other side, you are welcomed by your spirit friends. Their world is a natural world with houses, trees, etc. You don't change immediately. All is as you were when you entered the world of spirit. In your new life you go from grade to grade, but there are no materialistic worries."

And so we ended another session of classes. Mag and I went to Colby the next Sunday and as I passed Don Zanghi, in the back of the church, he signaled me. "When are you scheduling your office visit? You certainly haven't <u>forgotten</u>, have you?"

"No, I'll call you next week to set a definite time," I replied.

And I called the next week and made the appointment for January 28th. How was I to know this was probably to be the most significant day of my life.

I thought of the appointment and Don Zanghi, and as I thought, the desert scene I had visualized once again flashed through my mind. This time I looked at the girl. She had dark hair and was young. I could not see her face clearly. But she was so familiar...so very familiar. Then there was Don staring at her, smiling at her. As I viewed the scene I could sense his intense interest. Somehow I knew—just knew he would see her again.

I walked to and fro in my living room. I picked up Bear-baby, my smallest cat. "Tell me Bear-Bear what am I to make of these visions, surely of the past? I squeezed her playfully, but in her silence she kept her ancient wisdom to herself.

I thought again of January 28th. Would I find the answers to some problems in my life? Would I find out what the visions of Donald Zanghi signified? Good grief, could I even be hypnotized? I had to stop these thoughts; they were running like a caged squirrel in my mind. I would get some answers on the 28th. The cosmic joke was that Don and I both got more than we had bargained for!

9

The past-life regression

The morning of January 28th. I put on white jeans and a romantic, frilly blouse. I, naturally, topped it off with one of my wide-brimmed hats. Was I ready for this?

The sky was a beautiful shade of electric blue and the winter day was balmy as I made this—another journey this one to Deland to the office of Donald Zanghi. He had given me directions via the telephone. Hypnosis is not used on the spiritualist camp grounds. The mediums there do not use it for past life regressions. But Don uses light hypnosis and therefore keeps an office in Deland for that and for his massage therapy.

I passed the Farm Bureau offices; what if I can't be hypnotized? I do have a pretty scattered focus; my car wanted to turn at the Cassadaga sign, but onward to Deland. I could feel my heart doing its fast kettle-drum symphony. What would come out of this regression? Would I really learn something of past lives? Would I feel like I was living in another lifetime? How would that relate to my life now, to my problems now? Anticipation and dread: twin butterflies floating in my stomach. Several turns, a small lake, then the town proper; past the Union Bank to the public parking lot as directed. Fifteen minutes early; walking up the street and discovering <u>the</u> building; fifteen minutes early; I popped into a gift shop. Distraction—fear—anticipation were mixed with the gifts I handled, put down, scrutinized. 11:30, and across the street, up the stairs, to a chair outside the office door.

I heard footsteps on the stairs. "Oh", Don looked surprised, "I usually arrive <u>before</u> my clients." He opened the door and ushered me to the seat beside his portentous desk. The wall behind the desk was <u>covered</u> with certificates and credentials.

He wrote down the essentials of address, telephone etc. for his files. Then he sat back and searched my face. "What do you think this will be like, Jeanette?"

"1 just hope I remember what I say if I'm hypnotized!"

"This won't be deep hypnosis—you'll recall everything very clearly." What a relief—I didn't like the idea of blurting out things—perhaps private things—then not remembering.

"Tell me about your life, perhaps something you ponder over, perhaps some problems you need to understand."

Oh, dear, I thought, all my recurrent patterns that I kept repeating and repeating. "I've actually done many things in my life: a columnist for a weekly paper, boutique owner, restaurateur, English teacher, insurance agent—plus being a wife and mother. And now retirement and my younger lover. But"

He raised his eyebrows—"The problem?"

"The problem has been the <u>search</u>. I've never been really content with any man. Something missing. When I was very young I liked older men (intellectuals), and now that I'm older I like younger men (lusty).

He smiled as if he really understood. "And I always seemed to choose men I couldn't get involved with on a permanent basis. He asked the name of my former husband (Winston), and of my lover, Peter.

"More problems?" He queried.

"Yes, yes, I feel, lately, that I should be doing something—writing—helping people—something. I feel like my talents and my purpose are <u>tarnished</u>. I feel so afloat and useless." "Is there any information in particular you want from this regression?"

I didn't know where the courage came from. I don't know how I dared disclose it. "Yes, I want to know about the recurrent picture I see in my mind—the vision of a desert scene and YOU in armor with a band of soldiers."

I think he dropped his pen. "ME?" He asked. "You saw ME in this vision?" Astonishment was written on his face.

I was amazed at my courage, that I could tell him of the picture that kept flashing into my mind ever since I had said I would be regressed. The picture puzzled me, but was so real. At times it seemed as real as the now and the here.

He continued to look disconcerted as we arose to enter the inner sanctum. I don't think a client had ever seen HIM in a vision prior to a visit.

As I stepped through the door, I exclaimed, "Oh, I feel an energy in here." And, yes, I did feel an elevated energy in that room. Candlelight glowed, there was the thick scent of incense, the double window was deeply draped. I think there were celestial wall hangings. I noted shelves, side tables, a massage table in one corner (he is also a masseuse), and a recliner for the client.

He invited me to sit, relax, take a few deep breaths. He held his hand (palm toward me) in front of me and nearly above my head. He instructed me to keep focused on his hand as he brought it slowly closer and closer. "When I touch your head, you will close your eyes and be deeply relaxed. You will then focus on my voice. My voice is your focus. In the background you may hear cars, clocks, bells, but it doesn't concern you. Your only concern, your only focus, is my voice."

Yes, I thought like a deep meditation. My eyes were closed, perhaps I could open them, but I did not desire to do so. I just wanted to follow the voice.

"Jeanette, I will say certain words, and you tell me what you see—what pictures you see."

He said, "Winston."

I looked in my mind and it was blank and black.

He said, "Peter." Surely, my lover would conjure up a picture. But my mind was once again a blank.

He said, "Romantic love," and I drew another blank.

He said, "Lustful love."

It was blank again. Blank at romantic love and lustful love! Some small part of my mind said, "This isn't working."

Then he pulled the rabbit out of the hat.

"See _my_ face in front of you. Keep looking at my face. Now go along the time line. Choose a time. Keep looking at my face. Find the tunnel. Go through the tunnel to the time you have chosen. When I count to three—you will be there. One-two, three—your feet are on the ground."

I was smiling; I know I was smiling.

"Where are you? What do you see?"

I started to speak. What was this strange voice? This voice that spoke so slowly with such _effort_? It is _my_ voice, I thought.

I could hear the sound of the autos outside the building, but my focus was on a mental picture. I was in the picture, and at the same time observing the picture.

"Jeanette, what do you see?"

I'm standing beside the road. Soldiers—soldiers, bright armor—horses—I think horses."

"What are you doing?"

"Watching, watching, the soldiers—the armor, the horses."

"What do you look like?"

"Young, black hair, very beautiful,"—and all the time I had been the girl in the recurrent vision.

"What are you wearing?"

This seemed more difficult—the focus wasn't on me, but on "the" soldier. "I think sandals—a long dress". It was with a genuine effort that I spoke, and I could hear my own voice very low, almost inaudible.

"And what are you noticing?"

"Him—you. I'm looking at _you._"

"What do I look like?"

I smiled and thought God-like. I said, "Larger than life, a helmet, armor."

"What's happening now?"

"You turn, you look at me. The connection—the connection."

"What connection?" Don queried.

"When you looked at me—the connection—the recognition—I knew you from some other time, some other place, and I once again recognized you—it was the connection, when our eyes met. And I knew you would return. The horses are moving down the road, I see the dust. Yes, you will return."

"Did I return?"

"Yes, I'm in the house alone. A strange little house. Small like a bungalow, thick walls, rounded door. Suddenly you appear in the doorway. I go to you. I go to you."

"Do you want to tell me what's happening?"

I smiled. "No."

"Do you want to stay there a while?"

I nodded yes, and stayed there in that small house with Don for wonderful moments in time.

"Do you want to go on now?"

I nodded.

"You are on the time line again. Choose a time that is important to you. One, two, three, you are there."

I saw her—it was me again. "An Indian? A tepee!" I exclaimed.

"What do you look like?"

"Young, black hair braided, dressed in leather. I'm cooking over an open pot. I'm worried, apprehensive. I cook to keep busy because I'm worried about <u>you</u>. You are not there, but I know you are in grave danger."

"Do you know where I am?"

"Not exactly. But in my mind I see you, jumping, jumping high in the air, you wear leather with fringe, you jump and the wind blows your clothes around you." I don't see you <u>land</u>. I'm <u>worried,</u>"

"Do you want to stay here?"

"Oh, no, no, no!"

"Continue along the time line. Choose another time and place. One—two—three. You are there."

"England, I am in <u>England</u>.

"What do you see?"

"A house—a Tudor house." I could see the very large, tall, house, in a village. It had many gables, and some strange wooden decorations up on the gables that looked like wooden slats. "It is our house. It is where we lived." I did not see <u>inside</u> the house.

"What are you doing now?"

I saw an English field aglow with bright sunshine. Don and I were walking across the field, the field of colorful wild flowers and gentle slopes. We walked with two small children. Oh, my God, our children a boy and a girl. And the sun shone—the sun focused on the little girl. I was holding her hand. The sun shone on her golden yellow hair. And in that moment my heart ached and yearned for this golden child.

"What are you doing?" Don again queried. And before I could tell him about that particular scene, I immediately saw another scene. It was another day, but the same field of wildflowers.

"You and I are laughing and running in the field of wildflowers. It is somewhere near our house. I am wearing a long dress, and you have on some kind of tight trousers and a shirt with puffy sleeves. You catch me (I started to giggle), and you wrestle me to the ground. I smell the grass, the earth.

"You are on the ground with me. You look into my eyes."

"Do you want to tell me about it?"

"No."

"Do you want to stay there a while?"

"Yes," and I know I smiled. And there were more wonderful, remembered moments in time.

And finally, "Do you want to go on?"

"I'm tired, so tired."

"Jeanette, we are going to ask your higher self for some answers. There is a bright light going from your head-up-up to your higher self. You will go up the light to your higher self."

"Are you there? He queried.

"I don't know—I think so."

"I think you are there. Ask your higher self what significance all this has to you in the present. Do you know?"

"I don't know."

"You <u>will</u> know, later you will know. What have you learned about you?"

"I am the handmaiden."

"What did you discover about me?"

"The search is over—the connection—the other half." And I thought SOULMATE, SOULMATE, SOULMATE, through all our lives SOULMATE.

There were more questions and more answers—but somehow they have gone from my present memory.

He said, "You will be coming back now. You will awake refreshed. You will feel wonderful. I will count and when I reach three you will open your eyes."

And I opened my eyes—and it was wonderful. He smiled at me with a look of awe and I smiled at him. It seemed like thousands of years had passed since I stepped into this room from his office. He wasn't a mere acquaintance, but someone withwhom I had spent whole lifetimes.

"What are we going to do about this, Jeanette?"

"I don't know, I don't know."

10

That moment in time (a miracle)

I AROSE FROM THE CHAIR. "AFTER ALL THAT, AFTER ALL THOSE PAST LIVES, I THINK I DESERVE A HUG."

HE TURNED, HIS BACK WAS AGAINST A TABLE, AND HE REPLIED, "YOU CERTAINLY DO."

I WENT TO HIM AND SIMPLY PUT MY ARMS AROUND HIS NECK AND GAVE HIM A NICE PLATONIC HUG.

OF A SUDDEN, WE WERE LOCKED INTO AN UNEX-PLAINABLE ENERGY.

WE WERE STANDING THERE TRANSFIXED, WITH AN ENERGY FORCE CHARGING THROUGH US. I INSTINC-TIVELY KNEW HE WAS FEELING EVERYTHING I WAS FEEL-ING. THIS TRANSCENDED ANY HIGH OR ELEVATED FEELING LIFE HAD EVER HANDED ME. THIS WAS A LEVEL FAR SUPERIOR TO ANY SEXUAL ENERGY. WAS THIS ELEC-TRICAL—MAGNETIC—WHAT?

I DO NOT HAVE THE WORDS TO DESCRIBE THAT FEEL-ING: BLISS, ECSTASY, EUPHORIA—DO NOT DO IT JUS-TICE. IT IS SAID THE GURUS OF INDIA,WHO REACH A CERTAIN ELEVATED STATE OF GOD-CONSCIOUSNESS, USE HAND GESTURES TO DESCRIBE THE STATE—FOR NO HUMAN WORD COULD SUFFICE.

HOW LONG DID I STAND THERE WITH MY ARMS AROUND HIS NECK?

SECONDS, MINUTES, I DO NOT KNOW. THE SENSA-
TION CEASED, AND I NOTICED HIS KNEES WERE VISIBLY
SHAKING. I FELT NEAR COLLAPSE. "DO YOU KNOW WHAT
THAT WAS?" I STAMMERED. CERTAINLY, I THOUGHT, A
MEDIUM WOULD KNOW.

HE WAS HOLDING THE TABLE, STILL SHAKING," I HAVE
NEVER EXPERIENCED ANYTHING LIKE THAT."

"DO YOU BELIEVE IT WAS SOMETHING ELECTRICAL?" I
QUERIED.

"I THINK IT WAS ON THE SOUL PLANE", HE WHIS-
PERED.

AND I THOUGHT—"YES, YES, YES" THAT IS WHAT YOUR
SOUL FEELS WHEN IT CONNECTS WITH IT'S SOUL MATE.
I HAD BROUGHT BACK THAT ENERGY. I HAD BROUGHT
BACK THE ENERGY OF OUR PAST LIVES. WE HAD RECON-
NECTED OUR SOULS. IN CONVERSATIONS WITH GOD
NEALE WALSH SAYS ONLY OUR GRANDEST FEELINGS
COME FROM GOD. THE GRANDEST FEELING IS ONE OF
LOVE. AND SO WE HAD COMMUNICATED WITH GOD
THAT DAY OF JANUARY 28, 1997. THIS WAS TRULY MY
AWAKENING—MY BIBLICAL REBIRTH.

11

The immediate aftermath

Don began putting papers away, and snuffing out the candles. I was still transfixed, but had the presence of mind to ask, "Could I buy you lunch?" I knew I couldn't leave him yet, and as he answered in the affirmative I knew he felt the same way.

Before we left the office, he grabbed my hand and said, "Jeanette, Jeanette, what are we going to do about this?"

"Do you really <u>want</u> to do something about it?"

He cupped my face and looked into my eyes and replied, "Yes, yes, yes." And with those words singing in my heart we floated out of the building and down the street to a cafe. The cafe was located on the second floor; we stepped into the elevator. Before I could think, he had backed me against the wall and had his arms around me—his head lowered towards me and I thought, "Oh God, at last the kiss." It must have been what I had wanted from the first day I saw him, what I had wanted, but that which had been forbidden. Now, it was not forbidden, it was the <u>time</u>, it was the <u>place</u>. And we kissed, and we kissed, and time stood still for us—until the elevator stopped. "I wish this elevator could go on forever," he whispered as we stepped into the restaurant foyer.

Don't ask me what we ordered, don't ask me what we said. I remember the waitress taking the order, I remember we did talk, but mostly I recall I was still in the aftermath of the soul-touching. My mind and body were on a higher plane. And at times I could see his body quiver. We were in a special afterglow. Then we were again in the elevator, and more kissing, and out onto the street and walking towards the parking lot and my car. "I am so weak, "he said, "look my legs are still shaking."

"And I still need your arm to lean on," I laughed. The car was in a secluded spot at the far end of the lot. We leaned against the door and our lips met again. "Don't go," he pleaded.

But I knew, somehow I knew, this was not the time for anything else. "This is not the time," I replied, "we have had everything that was meant to be today."

He laughed, "You're stronger than I am. I'll call you when you get home." And there was another long kiss. He walked out of the parking lot as I drove out. I looked up the street and saw the familiar gate of his walk. And I felt I had left half of me with that bearded man walking down the street.

The car took me out of town; my mind was on automatic pilot. I could see Don in my mind's eye walking down the street; I could feel his arms around me, feel his kiss on my mouth. I could not believe this had happened. All the things I had secretly wanted had come true. I had never known any man this close to God. I had at last met the renaissance man. What was I doing in this car—my soul had wings I should be able to fly homeward. The trees passed my line of vision. Trees, trees, guess what has happened? This man said he wanted to do something about us—a relationship. Where would this lead? My mind grew dizzy at the thought. My heart simply sang and sang all the way home.

12

I research our past lives

I wonder if I dreamed that night, if I did the dreams must have been joyous. I awoke to a sunny day. My morning coffee seemed like ambrosia. I stood with the cup in hand and gazed out the glass door at the trees, torrid in the sun's warmth. As with most writers I "felt" words forming in my mind-I felt the poem:

ODE TO DON

Suddenly I am in total harmony,
My skin is penetrated by the sun;
I am its radiant warmth;

My feet are rooted deep
In mother earth's seductive glow.
My head communes with a
Nebulous, distant cloud.

Why?

Because yesterday
You touched me, you touched me
You touched me,

And today
I am closer to
The face of God.

It was nine o'clock. I yearned for the sound of Don's voice. The phone rang. And there were the warm, harmonious tones of his 'Good Morning'."

"Guess what? I have a poem for you. A woman who writes you poetry!"

And we sent our thoughts back and forth, still feeling in touch with our soul's afterglow. And I invited him to dinner that weekend. And he said, "Yes, yes, yes."

I turned from the phone and Don's voice to the sunlit glass door. I had a new awareness. The Christian Bible says, "You must be born again." Truly, this had happened to me. I had lived three past lives that I knew of, had died, and had been reborn—and here I was AGAIN. I was born into a new awareness the day my soul touched another soul. That day was Jan. 28th at approximately 12:30. My purpose here has not been fulfilled. I think my purpose has something to do with Don-being with Don. We have come into each other's lives now for a reason. I am so at one with everything, all of nature. My skin actually feels tight on my body—I can't encompass "everything" at once. I feel like I am walking on air, full of bliss and euphoria. <u>My God-consciousness is elevated</u>.

I went from that thought to the mundane task of washing the dishes, but it was not mundane my very hands were in love with the hot, soapy water.

My friend, Maggie, came visiting that night and exclaimed, look at you—you are glowing—wait a minute—you aren't trying drugs are you?" I laughed at the thought, I was on the only true drug: the opiate of existence: God-Realization.

"So how did the past life regression go," she asked, "must have been great from your expression."

"Yes, I did discover three past lives."

Where were they?"

"As far as I could tell-Egypt, Early America, and England."

"Anybody from your present family there with you?" Oh, oh, Maggie was up to her old personality trait of "inquiry and investigation."

"No I didn't see present family members, but I really don't want to get into details, Maggie."

She pursued a different cord. "Was it easy to be hypnotized—Do you remember anything you said."

"Mag, it was <u>light</u> hypnosis: I can remember every word I said. Look, I'd really rather not discuss it now. You need a regression, maybe you would discover why you can't lose weight, or maybe discover what your goal really is."

"Yea, maybe I will one of these days." Her expression changed. A sadness came across her face. "Buffie must be sick, she is hiding under the bed, and she hasn't eaten for two days."

"Your cat hasn't eaten for two days?" Buffie was the proverbial light of her life. But Maggie didn't like doctors or Vets—she usually doctored Buffie herself.

"Maggie, this is no time to procrastinate, take your cat to the Vets tomorrow. A cat that doesn't eat is a sick cat." She looked disconsolate as she walked out the door. "O.K., tomorrow I'll take her." And so another day had ended. But this one was different, so different for me.

I arise early, five or six. It is not always voluntary as four hungry cats prowl outside my bedroom door. One is allowed to sleep with me. If it is Bear-Bear, a furry, diminutive female intellectual, she demonstrates ingenuity in awakening me. First it is jumping over me. Then it is jumping onto my belly or breasts. (Ouch) If I shove her off the bed she gets vindictive. She jumps up onto the vanity and pushes items on the floor. From the depths of my foggy brain I think I hear golden rings and bracelets clatter to the floor. The fog lessens as I hear a favorite doll wobbling back and forth. "Bear—Bear," I yell. She descends and I settle in the bed again. I hear her bound onto a vanity stool near the bed, then another jump to the night-stand near the bed. First, the clock lands on the floor, and finally the telephone follows with a loud clang.

"Mother of God", I say and leap out of bed to pursue her.

So the day begins.

After the five mouths have been satiated, I take my coffee to the living room and watch the TV news. The newspaper lands on the doorstep.

The usual routine: I head for the door and my paper when I am confronted by a vivid flashback. I stand traumatized. I am reliving the regression, but the picture was even clearer.

I stood by the road watching the horses. Was I standing behind a wall, a short wall, perhaps waist-high? It was a thick short wall in front of the house. I could see the troop of horses and soldiers coming from a distance. They began to pass, and the soldiers with their bright armor shining in the sun. Suddenly, you (majestic and powerful) turned your head, and your eyes, your eyes, your eyes. As I gazed back—the connection: the present, the past, the future were there in that powerful force flowing between us. I knew as you proceeded down the road, you would return soon. I watched the horses, could see their rear ends, could smell the dust they kicked up as they disappeared from sight.

I hung onto the TV, shaking. I started to walk—back and forth, back and forth thinking, "Oh, God, what is happening to me?"

I returned to the past again—the Indian scene. Again, I was over the pot cooking. I cooked to keep busy. Worried, worried, you were away, perhaps in danger. As I cooked I saw a vision of you, jumping high into the air. I saw your clothes blow about you, I did not see you land. I did not want to know—did not want to know.

I walk again and start to weep. I had chosen that scene in time. Why?

I was still weeping as the last scene of England replayed. I stood for a moment in front of our Tudor house. I could dimly see inside: the vast entry hall, and the stairs wending to the top floor. This was misty and dark and I couldn't see clearly. Then I was in the field with you and the children. We traipsed through the grasses, over the slopes, through the wild flowers. And I could see us (like a voyeur) silhouetted in the sun.

Such a happy family. The sun shone on my little girl's hair—the sun shone brightly on her golden hair—.

I walked, I sobbed, I was completely distraught. Partly here, partly in the past. <u>Torn,</u> <u>Torn,</u> I knew I could not endure this alone. I called Don.

"I'm seeing it again. I'm reliving the regression again. I don't know what to do," I sobbed.

Don's sleepy voice replied, "All right, sit down, just talk to me, just talk to me."

I told him, and wept as I recounted the events. When I recalled our little girl I sobbed uncontrollably.

"Oh Don, I loved her so much." The overwhelming feeling of my love for her again flooded my being. I was no longer an <u>observer</u> of us in the past. I was NOW experiencing my feelings of love for our daughter. Don's voice soothed me. He told me never to fight the flash-backs—to accept them and learn from them And when he knew I could handle the situation—he thanked me for sharing, and we said a loving good-bye. I looked around the Victorian living room and gazed at the dolls, dolls, dolls. I had (without any conscious reason) begun collecting dolls two years ago. Now, nearly 100 dolls dominated the townhouse. My friends, too, wondered—why?

Now I knew, I <u>knew</u>. In each face I sought the face of my little girl from the past. I was subconsciously trying to find her in <u>this</u> lifetime. And the dolls stared blankly at me, as I searched each eye for the love in my daughter's eyes. Suddenly, all the visions took on particular signifi-cance. The Egyptian vision showed me how we had first connected, soul to soul, in that lifetime. The Indian vision showed me how I had lost Don. And, the English vision showed our perfect family life.

I <u>know</u>: I <u>know</u> and I thanked God for the awareness, the connec-tion, the knowing.

The sun in its rosy glory flooded the glass door. I went to the win-dow and meditated. I thanked God for everything, including my dis-eased heart that continued to keep me alive. And from somewhere in my heart or head—from my inner ear—I heard, "<u>You are covered with mercy and grace.</u>" I felt a physical warmth come over me like a mantle glowing from the top of my head and down over my entire body. I felt such joy in my heart. I felt like a champagne bottle about to POP its cork. POP, POP, POP, and I would spew out in all directions. I went into the living room and sat. There was such a joy in simply <u>Being</u>. I felt extended and encompassing, at one with the universe.

The weekend and the dinner for Don were one day away. Why was I getting nervous about a dinner? This was silly, I had cooked for a husband and three sons for years. I had entertained for my husband's business associates. I had entertained family and friends at multitudinous gatherings. Why was I feeling like a silly schoolgirl? I had seen Don eat at the groove service: he loved food. Shoot, I had cooked for him in past lives. Yet, as I entered the grocery store, I was all aflutter.

Then the strangest thing happened: I didn't procrastinate at the meat counter trying to decide between chicken or ham. I went in a certain direction and put my hand on a magnificent piece of beef for a pot roast. I could already smell it simmering in its juice with the carrots and other veggies. I had to get potatoes; I went to the vegetable department. And, I thought, what, oh, what for dessert. I picked up the potatoes, deposited them in the cart, and went down another aisle. I went directly to the apples, and picked up the Granny Smith variety. An apple pie—I was simply led to making the apple pie. Later, Don told me that apple pie was truly his <u>favorite</u> dessert.

We talked the next morning and he confirmed our dinner date for that evening. A dinner date—with Don. All the impossible dreams were coming true. And I knew in my heart I planned something more than dinner. I wanted us to be as complete as we were in the past.

I visualized the table looking special. He had been living in his Cassadaga bachelor pad since December and here it was the first week in February. He could use a little glamour. I hummed as I selected a gold tablecloth, gold flatware, and the white gold—rimmed best china. I placed an angel candleholder and flowers in the center and then stood back and admired the result. I even hummed through the arduous task of pie—making. I loved the taste of my apple pie. I had loved Susie's pie. Susie was Dad's second wife, and she was always resentful of Dad's daughter. But I told her how delicious I thought her apple pie was, and she allowed me to sit through one of her pie-making sessions. Therefore, I am able to duplicate her efforts (everything except the amount of flour that landed on the floor and had to be swept and mopped up at the finish). My Mom makes great apple pie, but she adds cloves—and that is not my favorite spice. Later, the smell of the pot roast filled the air. The combination of the spicy pie smells and the sweet aroma of the pot roast sent my taste buds into orbit.

As seven o'clock approached, I approached my closet. I collect dolls, but I also collect clothes, so my task is always formidable—what to wear form this overwhelming collection. I wanted to feel cool (and I already felt flushed), but look smashing. I finally selected a long black, slinky skirt and topped it with a sleeveless gold-colored tunic (with a plunging neckline), and finished with golden jewelry and glittering sandals. I looked good, the dinner smelled fabulous, the doorbell rang, and I fell apart.

I gathered up the pieces of me, and went downstairs—held my breath for a second—and opened the door to Don. Oh, man of the fabulous eyes—dressed in dark attire sporting a bold print shirt and sports jacket. Oh, man of the fabulous eyes—enter my world.

He entered, gave me a light kiss on the mouth, encircled my waist and said, "You look beautiful, but God, woman, what is that delicious smell. Something smells like <u>real</u> food, what is it?"

But I wouldn't tell—just led him to the coffee table where shrimp canapes and a bottle of chilled wine awaited us. We just talked and talked and soon the entire plate of shrimp had disappeared. I had found a ravenous appetite too. I was delighted to have him in my domain, in my little corner of the world. He looked around, at the walls covered with my favorite paintings, wreaths, etc. "I relate to this," he said "I do a bit of collecting myself."

"And I suppose you really relate to all these dolls!" I laughed. I think he said something noncommittal on that one.

I entered the kitchen, and food was ready to serve. I called him to the dining room all glowing in the candle-light. "This looks wonderful," he told me, and we sat and we ate pot roast until I said to save room for the apple pie. And then he told me it was his favorite, and I told him how Spirit had led me to the apples.

I smiled as I watched him savor the pie. It was delicious: all sweet, yet tart, with spices smothering its entirety. I knew I would send home the remainder with him. Finally, we stood and he came towards me, hugged me, and said, "Thanks, it was special."

"Watch the TV a bit and I'll do a quick clean up," I said. And I hummed to myself as I put the dishes into the machine, and the leftovers in the fridge. I hummed in anticipation of the remainder of the night. Don was in my house, in my house. I remembered 'when I had first seen him—that night in Colby Temple with the candles all aglow, that night when I walked towards him and sat on the stool in front of him, and he used God's healing powers on me, and he became an important person in my life. I remembered, I remembered.

"I want to show you some photos," I said. I showed him pictures of my sons, the rest of my family, of vacation trips, and days of my youth. We listened to music, and talked and talked and talked. And I knew we would soon reconnect the past with the present. I wanted that, I wanted us to be complete in every way.

And with the same instinct we both stood; I took his hand—and led him up the stairs.

13

The book: the love story

I awoke in the morning to the ring of the telephone. "You never get up early!" I exclaimed to Don.

"I have a meeting, and besides I had to say hello to you before I left. How are you this morning?"

"I think you are being very cute—you know exactly how I am."

From that morning on, we always talked. Every evening he called to say good-night. It seemed to be a beginning—on this plane—in this life.

That day kept giving me flashes of the house I had lived in while we lived our past life in England…the house I had called a Tudor house.

Maggie visited that night. "Buffie is very ill." She had taken her sick cat to the vets. She had had this cat for over fifteen years. She began to sob, "Buffie has cancer. I guess she doesn't have long." I put my arms around her: I certainly knew what it was like to lose an animal. I told her I would be there for her when the time came. I knew she would have Buffie put down at some point.

I, then, told her about the flashbacks of the Tudor house. I described the house. "Wait, a minute," she said, "I have a book on American houses and I think I saw a house in that book that was based on an old English house." My heart leaped—could I actually <u>prove</u> the past lives through this house? Maggie ran home to get the book and I felt all tingly—maybe, just maybe, I could prove the regression.

She returned and plopped the book into my hands, "<u>Field Guide to American Houses</u> by Virginia and Lee Mcalister. I, looked in the index and found Tudor houses. I had not known there was such a thing as

Tudor houses prior to the regression. And <u>during</u> the regression I knew I lived in this enormous house with the peculiar wooden trim. And here it was in print—a Tudor house—a Tudor house. I turned to page 355 and began to read under <u>Eclectic Tudor 1890-1940</u>. This was the <u>American</u> Tudor. I read that the identifying features of the house were steeply pitched roof; universal side gable (less common front gable facade dominated by one or more prominent cross gables, usually steeply pitched, decorative that is not structural); half—timbering present on about half of examples; tall and narrow windows, usually in multiple groups and with multi-glazing; massive chimney, commonly crowned by decorative chimney pots; wooden wall claddening. "Early American styles based on <u>English</u> medieval precedents (Gothic, Revival, Queen Ann) were executed predominantly in wood, whereas principal walls with wooden cladding are uncommon on Tudor houses."

"Oh, Maggie," I said, "It really sounds like <u>my</u> Tudor house." I turned to page 356 and learned the American Tudor style is loosely based on a variety of early <u>English</u> building traditions ranging from simple Folk houses to late medieval palaces. I read about half-timbering, and this is what I recall vividly as I recall the gables. Half-timbering is decorative (i.e. false) mimicking medieval timer framing, and is a common detail. It was the detail that I most remembered. I could see the gables with the decorative slats of wood making a pleasing design.

I wept as I turned to pages 364, 365, 367 and 368. There were photos of American Tudors. "My house, my house," I thought. "Oh, Maggie, thank you, thank you. I have proof that I lived in England, proof through these pictures, proof because I had never heard of a Tudor house, and here are the American replicas." She hugged me good-night and it truly was a <u>good</u> night.

I soon found it would get even better. I decided to meditate, thank God, for the day and the new knowledge. As I began, I thought about the Tudor house and I asked to see inside the house. I became very tranquil, almost as if I were in Don's office. I began to see another flash of the past. I knew this was true, because I see myself in the scene as an indistinct person—the scene always dominates.

I could see the house. It was dark and foggy. I was in a horse-drawn carriage, and they seemed to be moving over a stone (cobblestone?) road. We stopped in front of the house. I could see myself get out of the carriage and enter a door (divided-type?) and I walked into a candle-lit foyer. I put my hat on an entry stand (I still love and wear hats). I looked into an ornate mirror. I noted a pretty blonde woman wearing dark velvet. Then I ascended a most peculiar (to me now) winding stairway with multitudinous open rungs. I saw myself going into a bedroom dominated by a enormous canopy bed (canopies are still my favorite). The bed had massive posts all draped in velvet, and appeared to be elevated or on a platform. I went into the room, did something at the dresser, turned, and went back down the stairs.

I entered a large room. A long library table resided beneath a row of windows. The opposite wall housed hundreds of books. A fire crackled in the fireplace. A high-backed chair was drawn close to the fireplace. And there was my husband gazing into the fire. I quietly went to him and smiled. I sat on the floor in front of him and rested my head on his lap. Don reached down and put his hand lovingly on my head.

My vision ended. I was so happy with him in that life. The phone rang, and Don called to relate events of his day, and I told him about my day and the vision of the Tudor house. We both knew the reality of that past life.

The next morning I began to think constantly about William Shakespeare. I wondered if I were going to get a past-life vision about him. I had been fascinated by his plays in my high school English classes. While others struggled with the old English and the meaning; I seemed to understand Shakespeare's mind and feelings.

Later, at Adirondack Community College, I took Dr. Rogers' class. Once again, I was in love with the Bard. Dr. Rogers allowed me the privilege of reading her Masters: I was inspired. I knew that if I went for my Masters it would be Shakespeare. The class made a field trip to

Connecticut, and we watched a live theatre comedy. His bawdy sense of humor is in perfect attunement to my bawdy sense of humor.

I began to wonder if I had lived during Shakespeare's time in England. The Tudor period was from 1485-1603. And I'm sure those houses were of an enduring quality. I went to the dictionary and found that Shakespeare's birth and death dates were: 1564-1616. That's when I lived—that's when I lived in England. I felt it in my very bones.

The following Sunday, at the Temple, Homer Smith gave me a message reading from the pulpit. He told me I would need help with a project. He informed me that I should not be afraid to ask for that help. I was totally confused by the message. One can usually relate events of the present or past to the message, but this one confounded me. What kind of a project? And what would I need help with? And who, for heaven's sake, would I ask for help. But little do we mortals know. It was the future and the message would prove to be accurate.

Don had convinced me that we should keep our friendship under wraps. So I did not confide in my relatives or in my friend, Maggie. He was a candidate for his mediumship papers at the Camp, and didn't want anything to rock the boat. Wasn't it enough that his marriage was in a state of disintegration; there must already be speculation about that. And so we would "play it cool" for the time being. He promised that it was only a matter of time before we could reveal our true relationship.

So, life at Camp became a little difficult for me. I was a good actress, but hiding my feelings for Don was the ultimate test. However, I could see him enjoying this little cat and mouse game.

I walked into lyceum, and saw Don near the kitchen door, getting his usual coffee. He walked towards Maggie and me, "You look mighty handsome, Mr. Don," I chirped.

"And I certainly can say that hat becomes you," he retorted. "And how is Miss Maggie this morning? He continued with the game.

We sat in a circle awaiting D. Harold Warren, the lecturer. And when the attention of all was riveted on Dr. Warren, Don gave me a broad wink and raised his eyebrows appreciatively at my rather short skirt. I wanted to howl with laughter, but again had to play it cool and stifle my laughter.

Dr. Warren was to speak about an early spiritualist researcher, Sir William (Dr.) Crooks a British scientist. He told of the Fox sisters here in America about 1848 who witnessed physical phenomenon, but said that much began in Europe. He spoke of ectoplasm as the energy source for spirits. Ectoplasm is an actual substance drawn from people. It is a part of protoplasm in the human cell. It goes in stages of density—physical, ethereal etc. It is possible for the ectoplasm drawn from people to go to the spirit form and drape it so the spirit form can become visible, so all present could see the spirit form at the same time. Then, Photographs could be taken of the spirit form.

Dr. Crooks heard of the British medium, Florence Cook. Mrs. Cook had a spirit guide called Katie King. Katie was called the control. To a certain extent Mrs. Cook would turn her body over to the entity. This entails trust. Mrs. Cook could materialize Katie King with the lights on for all to see. Red light is often used as it does not disintegrate the ectoplasm. Mrs. Cook would sit in a draped cabinet to give privacy and where the ectoplasm could concentrate. To test Mrs. Cook, she would be tied with ropes to a chair. Yet, Katie King could appear from behind the cabinet in flowing white robes. Dr. Crook became interested in this apparent phenomenon.

The electron tube had been invented and it was thought the question of Spiritualism might be settled with this objective proof. Crooks was amazed at the spirit of Katie King. He photographed the spirit of Katie King and walked with the spirit (1874). He looked behind the curtain at Mrs. Cook. He passed electricity through her with a galvinometer. The needle did not move, and Mrs. Cook did not move, and yet Katie King had materialized outside the curtain. So Dr. Crook went on record about the authenticity of Mrs. Cook. He felt he had proven life in another dimension.

The spirits cannot remain long, as their vibrations are higher. Dr. Warren felt that in this present age, we really <u>could</u> have even more superior tests to prove, phenomenon in spiritualism.

As Maggie and I walked away from the Davis building, I looked back at Don. These words came to me:

> I suffer a mini death at each departure,
> Not hearing your voice,
> Not seeing your face,
> Not touching your hand,
> And the small aura of
> Death lingers
> And haunts me
> Until I see you again,
> And am reborn.

We wended our way home. I thought of the past life regressions, of the present, and wondered what miracles fate had in store for me. I knew there would be miracles. I leaned back in the seat, and savored the wonder of the universe…

Monday was not a good day for Maggie. She took the day off and we prepared to take Buffie to the Vets. I knew how she felt; I had put so many little furry ones to sleep during my life time. It feels like you are playing God with no right to do so. But, you carnot let the little creature suffer unnecessarily when you have the power to halt such suffering.

It is, indeed, a Catch 22. We entered her car, and I said, "Do you want me to hold Buff?" She declined, and put Buffie on her lap. She drove with one hand, and stroked Buffie with the other. She is like my sister, a "Masculine" driver. My sister began driving at an early age, and drives fearlessly, with great authority. Such is Maggie's driving. They both like speed. But, somehow one isn't afraid to be a passenger, as they exude self—confidence. And so she stroked Buffie as we zipped along to the vet's. She crooned and talked to Buffie. My heart was breaking for her.

We arrived at Dr. Bryant's office and were immediately ushered in. He is an older man who has suffered through many of these procedures, and still offers his love and sympathy to the pet owner. Mag held Buffie as the solution was prepared. I held Maggie. And then the worst time, as Dr. Bryant had to try repeatedly to find a vein in the shaved leg that would hold up. I sighed as he finally found the right place, and the procedure began. Maggie crooned to Buffie letting her know she would always be with her. A part of Maggie was being ripped apart as this animal of her heart was being put out of its misery. I hugged her tighter as Buffie's breathing stopped. Dr. Bryant assured her Buffie was gone. It was all over in a matter of a few minutes. He told her to stay with Buffie as long as she liked. The tears were flowing down her face as she stroked the body and crooned. "Remember, Mag, what we learned in lyceum, that cats are part of a group soul, and Buffie is now a spirit cat. She truly isn't dead." I left Mag to be alone with Buffie and returned to the waiting room.

Maggie would come from work tomorrow and find no furry friend to greet her. Maggie would suffer for a long, long time. I had recommended she start looking for another kitten soon. True, no cat can replace another, but the actual nurturing of a kitten helps mitigate the loneliness. Why did Maggie have to go through this? Wasn't her life sterile enough? No boyfriend—just work, and a few friends. Was this fair? I knew there had to be a reason for all this—past karma—something. But, God, please give Maggie a break. I waited a half hour. This wasn't good—she did not want to part with that still warm little body. She had made arrangements to have Buff cremated and ashes put in a marble urn. She would have her shrine.

I walked in, and she was hovered over the table with Buffie cradled in her arms. "Oh, Maggie," I said as I held her. I noticed a poster behind me and started reading it to her:

THE RAINBOW BRIDGE

There is a bridge connecting Heaven and Earth. It is called the Rainbow Bridge because of its many colors. Just this side of the Rainbow Bridge there is a land of meadows, hills and valleys with lush green grass.

When a beloved pet dies, the pet goes to this place. There always is food and water and warm spring weather. The old and frail animals become young again. Those who are maimed are made whole again. They play all day with each other.

There is only one thing missing. They are not with their special humans who loved them on Earth. So, each day they run and play until the day comes when one pet suddenly stops playing and looks up! The nose twitches! The ears go up! The eyes stare! And then that pet suddenly runs from the group.

You have been seen, and when you and your special friend meet, you take him or her into your arms and embrace. Your face. is kissed again and again and again, and you look once more into the eyes of your trusting pet.

Then you cross the Rainbow Bridge together never again to be separated."

Maggie gave Buffie a final embrace, and I led her from the room. "Let's go have coffee." I said, "This has been a tough morning and Buffie is probably tagging right along with us." She smiled through her tears at the thought of her little spirit companion.

I called Don and told him about the experience with Buffie. We talked about animals and group souls, how some animals may even progress to become human souls. I turned the subject to his birthday, the following Saturday. "Would you have dinner with me; I'd love to take you to some place fancy—have a real celebration?" He said he thought possibly, but he would let me know. I wondered if he were waiting for another invitation—from the family he had just lost or—from another woman—or I stopped there—the thoughts were getting painful. The next day he phoned and accepted my birthday invitation.

I was all aglow with the prospect. I would bake a yellow cake and decorate it with grandma's walnut frosting. This was a recipe that had been in the family for generations. It contained a secret ingredient that few people ever guessed. Plus, it was scrumptious! I baked the cake and put it in the freezer. I would make the frosting on Saturday morning. My heart hummed through the remainder of the week.

I agonized over wardrobe indecision's Saturday night. I finally had the hair looking really glamorous. A quick look in the mirror told me the black swirly-skirted dress of the new "slinky' material had been the right choice—especially highlighted with a rhinestone and pearl choker necklace. All my efforts paid off as I opened the door to Don's knock and he exclaimed, "My God, you look absolutely beautiful. I'm 48," he lamented. Forty-eight, I thought, wouldn't I love to be forty-eight again. I certainly wouldn't bemoan it.

I had chosen a new Italian restaurant that had it's opening tonight. I had made the reservations, but upon entering, there was still a slight wait for the table. People lounged on benches and some milled about. This was Don's milieu-he soon had the receptionist and half the people laughing at his jokes. He loved people—and he also loved being the center of attention. "If you don't behave, I'm going to announce your age," I threatened. The hostess rescued us before I got the opportunity.

We were soon wolfing down the wonderful bread we dipped in an olive oil mixture. We talked and each time the waiter asked if we wanted more Don was quick to say yes. Somewhere in the conversation with our young man, it was revealed he was a marshal arts student. Don glowed because he had owned a school, and was an accomplished black belt. After our order was placed, Don headed for the rest-room and I saw him stop our waiter, talk intensely, and then demonstrate some particular movement to him. Oh, Lord, he still misses his students, I thought.

The entree was delicious. I looked around at the opening crowd, all dressed for the occasion. A small-private dining alcove was to our left. I would have enjoyed that, but I'm sure Don preferred this center table where his all-seeing eye could view everything.

We suddenly found ourselves in more serious talk. I told him I was sure he must contrast this birthday with last year's, when he was surrounded by a family. And he said he missed the children—he had never adopted them legally—but had done so in his heart.

We talked of the separation and I asked when the divorce would be final.

"Oh," he said,' We haven't gotten around to that yet. There isn't any rush, and will start the proceedings when the time seems right." I know I became silent. He reached across the table and touched my hand, "What's wrong?" He queried.

"You are legally married. And I just couldn't tell my family—especially my Mom that I'm dating a married man. I'm sorry, I just can't date a married man."

He looked into my eyes and smiled. "I didn't realize you felt like that. I'll call, and start the divorce proceedings next week." It was that simple. The remainder of the time in the restaurant flew by like a dream. He would do this for me—speed along a divorce—because he wanted to date me. Because I had been his love in past lives—because I was important to him now.

We were both gorged on the birthday dinner, but at home lit the candles on the birthday cake and we ate a miniscule piece.

And I did not allow the birthday boy to leave my house until the wee hours of the morning.

14

The trip

I awoke to Don's call on Monday. "Good Morning," he crooned in my ear. Then we were off and running on a thousand topics. We talked about his heavy work-load; he was now into intense work for his mediumship certification. We talked, as it seemed we always did, about the past-life regression, of what we could have done in our lives in Egypt, England etc.

I bemoaned the fact that I was younger in all the past lives. "Why do I have to be older than you in this life? Maybe God does have a sense of humor. What if I had been gray, and obese, and you had experienced these feelings for that woman?" I smirked.

He broke up laughing at the thought, "Oh, there is a God," he howled.

"Wait," I said, and read him a poem I had written about the regression.

"Jeanette," it just came to me that you should keep a record of all the events and thoughts about what has been happening to you."

A record I should write about this, a record, I should write about this, a record, I should write about this…. I knew, I KNEW, I KNEW. I should write a BOOK about this. I would write a book about this. A BOOK…A BOOK…. A BOOK.

And that was the moment this book was born.

When I hung up the phone, I went immediately to my desk and found a pad of lined yellow paper. I began to write the events of the past-life regression. I was swept away into reliving the event, and suddenly found myself exhausted and at the end of ten hand-written pages. I immediately wrote about "That Moment in Time" when my soul touched Don's. I put the pen down and began to think about Spiritualism, how people have such misconceptions about it (my youngest son won't set foot on the grounds, thinking it is the devil's workshop). I wanted to shout to the world the truth about this religion. Where to begin? At the beginning, of course, my first trip to Cassadaga with Maggie. So I began an outline and ventured into the first chapter. My handwritten efforts would fall into the end of the book.

I had work—this was meaningful work. I set aside at least two hours a day to think about the book and to write, write, write. Sometimes I felt <u>unworthy</u> of the project. Who was I to think I was good enough to write about a religion? But I would go on. Writing is like being pregnant—you can't be a little pregnant—it is all-consuming. I would be watching TV, and a voice would fill my mind "Use the first paragraph of your introduction notes—use the remainder as flashbacks." I would snap off the remote, grab my notebook, record the thoughts. I thanked my writing guide. She hovered near. I am the <u>Channel</u> for this book, <u>I am worthy</u>.

I remembered the evening when the candles glowed in Colby Temple. It was mediums night. I recalled stopping at the table of medium, Phoebe Rose Bergin. She said I would be writing. And she said, as I walked to her table, she saw my writing guide with me. She saw her very skirts sweep the floor as she walked to the table with me. She was with me then, as she is with me now.

Later that week Don called, "How about a real date? How about a movie?" I was thrilled—he had actually asked me out—into the real world of Edgewater. He was so funny—he had his little ritual about the seating. "Here," he said, and then changed his mind about the seat and the side of the theatre. We wound up in the middle (with him in an aisle seat) on the far side. I later found he would never walk into a movie late—it just isn't right if you aren't 15 minutes early. When I was finally seated, he excused himself to get the popcorn. He came back with an enormous bucket and a gigantic drink.

"Are we feeding half the people?" I inquired.

"I love popcorn and there's nothing like movie popcorn," he informed me. He was also an affectionate companion—holding my hand and giving me a smile or a glance at significant parts of the movie. The movie: I don't remember it at all—I just remember our first "real" date and the fun of being with Don.

The book progressed and I was into Chapter two. I told Maggie about the book, and that Don was helping with the research. I, of course, did not divulge the true nature of our relationship. So Don showed up at least once a week, and I would cook dinner and we would go over the manuscript, and then just continue with our evening together.

Then it hit—my journey into depression. It was my journey into a private hell. I began to dwell on why I was older than Don in this life-time. What kind of cosmic joke was this: why hadn't he come into my life before? He was now like a transparency covering my mind. I saw all through the transparency of him: my other half.

I couldn't write—I was <u>blocked</u>. I crawled into a quiet place: it was my private hell. In <u>Conversations with God</u> it is said we create our own hell. Could I battle my way out and regain my joy in living? The battle went on, I had to find my truth again. Should I write Don out of the book as the soulmate? But that would be a sin of omission. Should I just dump the concept of the book? I finally had to talk to Don about it. I called.

"People have the strangest ideas concerning soul-mates," he told me. Your soul-mate usually comes back to you in a time of need. You came to me-were regressed and recognized our past lives together. You had given up the joy in living and felt you were not using your talents. I came back into your life in your time of need."

"Like the healing you performed. And when you said I should take notes about the regression. That was when the book was created...when our minds and souls met in this creative concept you planted the seed in the uterus of my mind-I would carry the book idea for months-labor, until it was brought forth into the world-published as OUR product-the product of an immaculate conception."

"That was our moment of conception, when the idea of the book was created by us," he agreed.

I wept and wept because I could see the truth of our union on this plane.

"Jeanette, when I help you, you receive joy in the awareness of God and in your creative writing. And when that happens to you, my soul is part of that joy."

And so I walked out of my hell and back to the world of writing.

That night I stood under the shower, the hot water coursing over my body, I raised my hands skyward and heard the words clearly in my mind, "You are the handmaiden of the Lord."

I went on with the book and Don was off and running. He has an avid interest in aliens and UFO's. There was a meeting at Gulf Breeze. He was taking the trip with his friend, Matt Kiss, and would be gone for several days. I tried to put on a brave face, not wanting him to know how much I would miss him. But he knew. We met at the house the night before he left, and when he said good-night, he kissed me and said, I'll call you every day." He called, talking of meeting old friends, beach groups looking for UFO sightings, the lectures, the special circle with Donald Ware, in which Don was privileged to participate. I missed him. My life seemed so incomplete without him. It had not felt this devoid before. I was doing the things I had done: visiting with Maggie, taking Mom to dinner, tending my cats—and now the addition of writing the book. But alas and alack—I lacked my Donald. Oh, yes, I was beginning to think of the Donald as my Donald. And one night when I was especially restive, I remember getting out of bed and sitting by the window looking at the moon and writing:

> I do not need to think about life and living
> And death and dying and Don and Peter tonight.
> I do not need to think of my sick heart
> And heart surgery and Don in my present

And Peter in my past tonight.
I do not need to lie under this canopy bed
With a huge black cat
Purring in my arms tonight.
Tonight, I would have Don in my arms
In the never-ending now that would dispel
The dead past and diseased heart.

And then he was coming home the next day and, of a sudden, I had the phone call late at night—he was back and he was sorry it was so late, but he had to touch in with me. And I wouldn't have cared if it were four in the morning. He was back, and my heart was full of song. Donald was home again.

We met the next day and went to a little Mom and Pop restaurant, The Eattery, for lunch. How was I to know this would be the most significant luncheon of my life? We were ushered past the cash register, and small tables into the main dining room. Another couple chatted up front near the window, but Don and I headed for a table in the rear. He ordered a Coke and I ordered coffee. The waitress left us in peace. "I missed you," he said.

"And you don't know how much I missed you," I smiled.

"Jeanette, what do you see for us in the future?" He asked.

And I had a vision of the future. "I see a house that we both love. I see us in the house. You will be a certified medium, and you will be doing that work, but you will also be helping people—lots and lots of people. I see you holding classes and coming home with groups of people for coffee. I see you being larger than life and I am happily a part of it. I see my writing—I also see me cooking."

He reached across the table and took my hand. Tears were welling from the sides of his eyes. I took his hand and tears flowed freely down my face. And we both knew, we <u>KNEW</u>, our future together was settled. We would be together and married in this lifetime.

We walked out of that restaurant with wings on our feet. Near the car he took me in his arms and whispered, "My girl."

We got into the car and drove around in a semi-trance. We talked of the future—perhaps in Cassadaga. A house in Cassadaga. Was this really happening to me? I'm sure I was glowing because as I looked at him—he was glowing. And we went to the ocean, sat, and meditated—thanking God for reuniting us on this plane.

I wanted to shout it from the proverbial roof—tops. I wanted to tell my family and Maggie. I wanted the people at Cassadaga to know. He did too, but we still had to wait, wait until his mediumship papers were finalized. I thought, why not tell now, but his divorce wouldn't be final until June—best to wait. He called the morning after the "Sock Hop," and he had danced up a storm with every gal available. And my heart was heavy that I hadn't been to the Cassadaga "Sock Hop." And the next night was the community dinner-and he shared it with a blonde newcomer—and again I felt sad that it wasn't me.

June 23rd was a banner day for me. That was the day my application for Spiritualism was accepted and I became a member of the Southern Spiritualist Camp at Cassadaga. I had sent in my letter and two spiritualists, The Rev. Thomas Berkner and the Rev. Nick Sourant signed my application. I wrote the customary letter explaining why I wanted membership:

To whom it may Concern—In retrospect, I believe I have <u>always</u> had spiritualistic tendencies. As a Catholic child I recall praying to the Saints, and lighting candles for relatives in Spirit. Later in life, I recall a searching, reading, studying because of problems with precepts in my religion—such as vicarious atonement. I returned to school and discovered more great ideas in philosophy classes. I had been toying with the ideas of reincarnation and now became convinced. Through books on Eckankar I discovered more truths on out-of-body, meditation, and the many planes of heaven. In 1996 I brought these truths with me to my first service at Colby Temple. I read the declarations, and found I had reservations about healing and mediums. I decided to explore. I have been attending lyceum classes regularly, have attended a healing class and lectures.

Healing has been proven to me by my healing from Donald Zanghi. Mediumship had been proven to me by a reading from Arlene Sikora, and several messages at the Grove and Colby₄ I can now read the declarations with belief in their veracity. As a Spiritualist I have the desire to live my life in the light of these principles of truth and beauty."

This was a date I would remember forever—June 23—like the other date I would always recall—January 28th when our souls connected in that Deland office. And that was the day I wanted to marry Don—January 28th. But fate would have it otherwise.

And then, out of the blue, Don was off and running again. He had been sitting at the Cassadaga Hotel having coffee with his friend, Matt Kiss, when Matt said there might be tickets available to fly to Machu Peechu. Don's ears became attuned. In a past life he had been a priest and had taken a group of students up the mountain. He walked ahead, and then turned to talk to the students. When he turned, he slipped, and fell off the edge, off the mountain to his death in that particular lifetime. Now, he had the urge to see the mountain in <u>this</u> lifetime. So when Matt suggested the trip he said, "<u>Yeah, let's do it.</u>" <u>These words are words to remember as they are linked to another event</u>. So he called to tell me he might be going to South America—to Peru—for a week.

And I wanted this trip for him, but I didn't want the aloneness for me.

He was packed and called. We had had a special good-bye dinner the prior evening. "I want a tape to play while you are gone," I had told him. He promised to drop it off before his departure. "I'm going to miss you so much. I know you can't call from there, you'll be on the go too much—and it is costly. But, God, I will miss you. I love you, Donald Zanghi."

"What did you say?" he asked. I had never before put it into words. And neither had he.

"I love You," I repeated.

"Say it again."

"I love you."

"Say it again."

"I love you."

And the conversation ended with my statement. I felt a little tear in my heart, as he had not expressed the same emotion.

The next day he left the tape for me, and we kissed goodbye. I watched the car depart and saw him wave a final goodbye. I couldn't wait—what kind of message would he leave?

I popped the tape in and waited:

"Honey, I miss you already, and I shall miss you every minute of this trip. But just think, in a short while you will be back in my arms again. Take care of yourself. I love you."

The tear in my heart condensed into sunshine: he loved me and he had put it on tape. How many times did I play that tape during that long week? Well, it's a wonder I didn't wear it out. I had apprehensive thoughts—would he retrace his footsteps up the mountain and fall off again? I knew he had had a cold when he left, would the altitude make him sicker—would he wind up in a hospital? But, where was my faith? He would be fine. He would see the ancient ruins that had once been his home in a past life. He could experience the Peruvian culture and mingle with the Peruvian people. He would find new taste sensations in the South American culinary efforts. He would be awed by the great stone artifacts—those ancient buildings so like the structures of the Egyptian pyramids. What would he experience in the great city of Cuzco? What kind of accommodations would he find? I had heard traffic rules were helter skelter—but knew he would remain safe. My thoughts were with him all week, my prayers were with him all week.

But the day of his return was near and I would be whole again.

He returned, now spouting "I love you," continuously. It was like the dam had burst and the torrent of words of love poured forth. The best thing that happened, upon his return, was the bestowing of his mediumship papers. Now that that was finally accomplished—we could concentrate on "us." At the 4th of July picnic, we could appear at camp as "a couple." I was excited, yet a little apprehensive. He had been seen with many women "friends" after his separation, but now a "girlfriend?" How would people react to this? Don said I was silly to fret about it; everyone would be happy for us.

As we walked down the grassy knoll towards the picnic area, Don held my hand. Thank God, they wouldn't mistake me for just another friend. Everyone already knew me, so there wouldn't have to be introductions. We walked from one group to another, chatting. I didn't see any eyebrows raise, but I'm sure we were giving them food for thought. Jean Sourant worked over a pot of food at the table and greeted us warmly. We filled our plates, and sat with one of Don's friends. We laughed and joked—acting like any couple in love. I am sure we left no doubts that we were "a couple."

Now I was invited to all of the social events. The following week the monthly camp potluck supper took place.

I had a new bread machine and decided to contribute a freshly baked loaf. Again I was apprehensive. This group was more intimate; the people in closer proximity. Again, we entered holding hands. We joined the food line, and Don spoke to a man I had never seen. "Oh, Dave, I want you to meet my fiance, Jeanette," he said. And several times that evening I was introduced as his fiance. I think we must have had a few heads buzzing—one week his girlfriend—the next his fiance.

15

The miracle tape

Two miraculous events were promised in this book. One was the reuniting—the actual touching of our two souls after the past life regression. The other I call "the miracle of the tape." The tape was the recorded reading of the message of Helene Liberte when I was searching for the truth of mediumship. We will flash back to chapter 4 when the details of the reading were revealed and the promise of a revelation and a message. Helene recorded the session and the only voices on the tape should have been Helene's voice and my voice. After the session she handed me the tape. I got into my car to return home, decided to drive through town, and lo and behold, there was <u>my</u> then <u>friend</u>, Donald Zanghi. I suddenly wanted to share the session with him. I stopped the car.

"Oh, this was the day of your reading with Helene, wasn't it?" He asked. I knew I had mentioned it to him at grove service and was flattered he had remembered.

"She sure proved the mediumship thing to me," I laughed. "She definitely brought through my ex-husband. There was no doubt there, he is just as concerned about my finances on <u>that</u> side as she was on <u>this</u> side. And my Dad came through as loving and kind as ever. But, here, would you like to play the tape and see what you think of the session?"

"Sure, I'll go in and play it now. I'm glad you got such a good reading. Have a safe journey home: I'll return the tape on Sunday." I waved good-bye to him and went directly home.

About a half hour after I returned home the phone jangled. It was Don. "Jeanette, if you aren't sitting down—sit down.'

I sat on the arm of the chair, as he continued. "Just you and Helene were in that room, right? I confirmed the fact. "But, are you ready for this? There is a <u>third</u> voice on the tape." No, I thought, that was <u>impossible</u>.

"But, only Helene and I were in the room, and so only Helene or I could be on the tape."

"Wrong. I was listening to it, and went through the first side of the tape and it was normal in all respects. Then I turned it over and was listening with the earphones, just lying back, relaxed, when I heard a <u>different</u> voice on it. I thought, wow, back it up, what was that? So, I took off the earphones and played that section again, and it was a voice and the message was very distinct. I was totally amazed. But, wait, let me get it and you listen and tell me what you hear." And so he held the tape recorder near his phone and played it.

I heard Helene's voice—"YOU ARE GOING TO VISIT THE SOUTHWEST. YOU ARE BEING DRAWN LIKE A MAGNET. IT WILL BE PRIOR TO 1999. THE TRIP WILL HAVE A SPIRITUAL ASPECT. YOU WILL BE GOING WITH SOMEONE.

And at this point another voice was heard. It said, "<u>YEAH: LET'S DO IT.</u>"

"Did you hear that? Did you hear that? I've played this about twenty times, on this machine and another. There is no doubt of this third voice. You did hear it didn't you?"

"Well, I can hardly believe my ears. It said, "<u>Yeah, let's do it</u> when she said I would be going with someone. Oh, God I don't believe this! This is like a miracle—a voice out of the blue on my tape."

"But, Jeanette, there's something else. Don't you recognize that voice? Wait, I'll play it again." And I held the phone to my ear tightly. He played the tape, and I listened. Yes, I knew that voice—I had just been <u>listening</u> to that voice, Oh, God, how could it be? There was no doubt in my mind—I knew the voice of Donald Zanghi and it was on my tape. Impossible! He was several blocks away and involved in some other project when my tape was being recorded at Helene's.

"It's <u>your</u> voice. I don't understand it, but it is <u>your</u> voice."

"Yes, that's one reason I'm so amazed. I give the lectures on physical phenomenon, and I know <u>spirit</u> voices come through on tape, but I've never known spirit to use the voice of the living in this manner."

"You think spirit did this?"

"It's the only explanation. Or my higher self from another plane coming down and manifesting on the tape."

"Then we have something very special here."

"I'm blown away by this. I can't wait to let Helene know. She will be blown away too."

And I thought of the fact that he was married (<u>then</u>), and that the tape had said "Yeah, let's do it." Let's go to the SOUTHWEST? He would be the person that would go to the Southwest with me? What kind of a bizarre thought was this? What was spirit trying to communicate?

"I want to come to your house and play this for you. I want you to be as sure of this as I am." And so I gave him instructions to my house. And we played and re-played the tape in awe.

Now I am his fiance. We know the message was to let us know we are meant to be together. The spirit world gives its blessings to us. It was also meant to prove the power of spirit to us both, and to absolutely prove mediumship to me. He now uses the tape in his physical phenomenon lectures!

16

Meditations and visions

The past life regression was spiritual rebirth. Don suggested I take a course in transcendental meditation, and I contacted his teacher, Laurence Topliffe. Meditation proved to be a key to getting in touch with the God within. I meditated twice a day in twenty-minute sessions. Many visions of the past and future floated into my mind.

I began to take special notice of seemingly accidental occurrences. I took my cat "CC" to the vets. While waiting for my turn, another woman crooned to her caged cat. We exchanged pleasantries about our felines. Her name was Marion Bishop. I don't know why, but I mentioned my fiance was also doing reike healing on the cat. Oh, she will think I am crazy, I thought. But, no, she smiled as I went on to mention that Don was a medium. "I attend the Northern Spiritualist Camp at Lillydale, N.Y." she laughed. There are no <u>accidental</u> meetings.

In one meditation I saw the Egyptian Karnack and Zozar temples and remembered getting that old familiar feeling. I suddenly sensed my "Egyptian" mother. I saw her robed figure.

I was a small child walking along beside her, holding her hand.

I knew I was a child, but could only envision my body, not face.

I knew she was not my present Mom. I shuffled along in the dust and heat holding her hand. Multitudinous bangles jangled on her arm then.... as the multitudinous bangles jangle on my arm <u>today</u>.

Later, I saw myself as a young and beautiful girl in a wondrous, headdress with what looked like a coiled snake representation on it.

I saw an image of Zozar's temple and there was Don in an Egyptian headdress walking up the gigantic steps.

In the shower I had heard "You are the handmaiden of the Lord." Had I, at one time, been a temple priestess?

My love of books, my love of writing showed up in another vision. I was reading from "Astara's Book of Life" by Earlyn Chaney. I read about the great fire that leveled the Library of Alexandria. Under instructions of Theophilus came the burning of the immense library of Alexandria in Egypt in the third century, from which tragedy the world will never fully recover…although some of the precious books and manuscripts were spirited away and saved. The renowned library contained over 700,000 of the most remarkable writings, documentaries, books, and manuscripts ever collected on the face of the earth. Although the great Library-Museum itself survived, its inner glory was ultimately destroyed.

I put my book aside. My chakras were glowing: my signal of great spiritual awareness and truth. I saw a dark sky, and in the near distance a great roaring fire painted the sky. It was the fire of the great library. I saw a figure near the library, a figure prostrate on the earth, a figure banging its head into the earth in sorrow. I was that figure. I had lived then, and had witnessed the burning of the books. I cannot describe the sorrow that engulfed me. I was as destroyed as the books. I banged my head into the earth wanting it to swallow me up forever. I came out of the vision with my face awash with tears. I wonder if my love of the written word has followed me through all my lifetimes.

I never knew what a host of angels meant until I had a vision during a meditation. At this point I wish I were a painter, so I could aptly describe the living painting I saw. It was like something from one of the old masters: an eternal and ancient quality. The colors were gold, black and white. In the center of the vision was a shaft of golden light. It was triangular in shape with the apex part at the top, narrowing down to the bottom of the light. From the center on down to the bottom angels—enormous angels—the cherubim—the seraphim were kneeling, swinging incense holders, chanting their praises to God—hosanna on the highest…glory be to God…the highest glory to God. These angels were detailed and clear. And from the darkness on the outer limits of the living picture specks of angels could be seen coming from all directions: from the East, from the West, from the North and from the South. The host of angels came from the darkness and into the golden light. The nearer they came, the more visible they became. The angels nearer the center took on form and shape. As they came near the golden light they kneeled and took up the chanting and praising of God. The host could not be counted: from the mere shadows or miniatures flying in from the darkness, to the forms in the shadows, to the visible forms in the Light, to the distinct forms <u>near</u> and in the golden light. Those near the light looked upward with rapt attention. This is a living picture that will dwell in my mind for as long as I am on this side of the veil, and perhaps throughout <u>my</u> eternity.

In meditation I had three sightings of the Master Jesus.

In one I saw him at a distance, in profile in a golden light. In another I saw his face and looked directly into his eyes. I will not try to describe looking into the eyes of Jesus. It would be like looking into the soul of the universe. The third scene was a direct contact. I had been hurt because one son refused to accept my Spiritualism, and would not set foot in Cassadaga, calling it the devil's workshop. My sorrow was deep, because I had always accepted whatever denomination he chose, I expected him to do the same. In meditation I was taken by my spirit guide to Jesus and I told him of my sorrow. He sat in a chair and took me on his lap, cradled and hugged my sorrow away. I still feel sadness over my son's decision, but the deep ache has disappeared. I have been comforted in the arms of Jesus….

Did I have a vision about my book? Yes, yes, yes, and it was when I was still just friends with Don. I saw the book cover, and to my bafflement the author was Jeanette Strack-ZANGHI. At the time I thought I had conjured up some wishful thinking, after all we were just friends. During that time period I had another vision. This one I thought quite preposterous as we hadn't even had a date. The focus of the scene was Don, all decked out in something black. He was looking at a woman with complete devotion—in the candlelight—in a church—in front of a minister. I turned my attention to the woman, I could only see a bit of lace, her back was turned towards me, but the woman, I knew that woman…I was the woman he was marrying. <u>Yes, I had the vision before our first date</u>.

I was puzzled about one meditation. I saw an office building: enormous. I was in an upper story room, the windows were long, overlooking a sea of other buildings. Someone from behind a desk was talking to me. I haven't figured out the significance of this except it may concern a <u>book</u>.

I have also been privileged to see the "river of time." If time is a device and we are traveling on that time belt I saw it. It was like a foggy stream and Don and I were holding hands traveling through time together.

I have also seen myself on the other side of life. In the spirit world I came to "the halls of wisdom and knowledge." The building was so tall one could barely see the top. Giant arched pillars, walk-ways, and indescribable gardens flanked the building. I don't think the human mind can encompass the enormity of the halls of wisdom and knowledge. The spirit beings moving about looked like ants in comparison to the building size. Spirit beings moved in and about the outside paths, near the gardens and under the enormous pillars. Inside, many advanced spirits could merely chose a book, hold it, between their hands, and absorb knowledge. I recall reading word by word for the pleasure of what I was learning. Then there were the classrooms. I sat in one of the smaller rooms with a handful of spirit people. A master teacher came into the room. The teacher must have been from a higher level of heaven, as his robes glowed with white light. No, I am not allowed to recall what he imparted to us.

When reading Astara's <u>Book of Life</u> one morning I began getting the chakra glow and started sobbing. "O.K., God what's up?" I thought. I closed my eyes and saw a rainbow bridge. It was a bridge surrounded by space and stars. This was a dazzling bridge of color seemingly the bridge between the physical and spiritual realms. I was flying up the colored column and I was holding someone's hand. I was not flying alone. The deep space surrounded us, the stars glittered. But my heart was happy. When Don had passed, I came from the spirit world to greet him. I held his hand and lead him to our true home, our home in Etheria, and our new venture into the halls of wisdom and knowledge....

I will share one more event. This happened during a circle, familiarly known as a seance. My writing guide came through. The spirit manifests by shaking the table the circle of people sit around. Through a series of questions the spirit responds by shaking the table for "yes," and letting the table be still for "no". My writing guide let us know she had someone with her helping me with the book. And again we questioned and found it was Elizabeth Barrett Browning. If my work suddenly gets a poetic twist it is she.

17

The final journey

I was still living at the town-house. I visited Don at his apartment in Cassadaga, and the town was aware that we were engaged. Aware, but quite surprised! He had told one of his friends he was engaged and she started playing the guessing game of who it could be. She must have guessed every unmarried gal in camp including some mediums. We had kept our relationship under wraps—absolutely no one guessed "me."

One night, Maggie, popped in to visit and my son, Wayne, was there. We were recalling the last time the eldest son, Winston, had visited from New York state and the good time we had. Wayne was now engaged to a gal who had a drinking problem. And he was still struggling with the fact that his marriage of sixteen years had dissolved—that his son was only a weekend visitor. Wayne is a frustrated comedian: most comedians always seem to have a tragic side. Maggie walked in—Maggie with her boisterous laugh and charming smile. Maggie walked in, sunshine followed. I can't recall who talked the loudest or laughed the longest. "God," I thought, "if these two aren't peas in a pod." I had never seen such similar senses of humor. They really liked each other, but he was now engaged to another.

We all said good-night. But an hour later I happened to look out the window, and there were Maggie and Wayne under the light of the street lamp still laughing and talking.

"Guess what? I think we may have a house," Don exclaimed vehemently into the phone the next morning. I couldn't wait. We could look at the house that evening.

We held hands as we rode into Cassadaga. "Honey, do you have a good feeling about our getting this house?" I asked this new medium. He squeezed my hand and grinned at me, signifying yes.

We were greeted by the owners Lois and Marie Gates, two students of Spiritualism. Marie always wears a smile, has a pretty face, and short-cut blonde hair. Louis is tall, muscular, and wears his smile well too. She hugged me at the kitchen door and confided, "We could have sold this to another, but I didn't <u>feel</u> the house wanted it." I wondered if she would feel the house wanted us.

I guess if I had had a career wish it would have been clothes design. But interior house design would have been a close second. I can always visualize a finished room. We walked into a large kitchen. Marie has a passion for bright colors and it reverberated with a bright, hot pink from the walls to the refrigerator. One wall was covered with white turn—of-the century cabinets. It was a big kitchen, a splendid kitchen.I had told Don I wanted a Chinese kitchen, an Egyptian bed-room, and other rooms Victorian. He complied, as long as he could have all his offices and rooms in the metaphysical mode. My kitchen, I thought, and saw it in white, with (Chinese) dark blue cabinets, and a Chinese red rug and all my pictures and statues in the that motif. I was thrilled, and I could see Don knew it. We walked into the dining room and it was an interior room in dark-paneled wood. Some light seeped in from the sun-porch, but it was altogether too dark. I knew it would be splashed in white and would house my drop-leaf table, and marble-topped furniture (plus a few dolls!) We turned left into an interior room the Gates used as a bedroom. This would be white with bur-gundy lace at the French doors—it would be all Victorian and it would be our living room.

The Gates then led us through the French doors into a room that had once been a wrap—around sun-porch. It now housed a desk and some wicker chairs, the walls were light pink. I could see it as my doll museum and writing room. I thought of Virginia Wolff with a "room of her own." This would be my room: a room where I could be surrounded by my little friends while I finished my book. Another turn took us into Marie's sewing room (part of the wrap-around porch). I could envision this as a guest room, but with a wrought iron table and chairs in front of the window—where Don and I could enjoy afternoon tea. It was sunny and bright, a garden room with plants and flowers, an indoor-outdoor feel. But what about the bedroom? I had already vetoed the idea of it between the living room and the sun-porch....no, that would be the living room. Then we were led off the dining room to a room now used for Reiki healing. The walls needed much repair, but I knew it could be done. It really was too small for what I wanted. Finally, Marie led us to a small parallel room off the sun-porch. It was narrow, dark with a closet at the far end. Voila! <u>Tear out the wall</u> and there could be one enormous bedroom. Yes, the huge bed with a pyramid canopy over it, the palms, the Egyptian wallpaper, the pictures, statues, tables of Egyptian memorabilia.... our <u>Egyptian bedroom</u>. The house was wonderfully big, upstairs housed an apartment. The renter was away that evening and the Gates took us on a tour. There were three big rooms and a sunporch. Suddenly I could see Don doing what I did downstairs-"seeing" how he would decorate his reading room (now the kitchen), his teaching room (now the bedroom) and the office (now the living room). I could see the intense gaze as he pictured all his metaphysical artifacts on walls and shelves. And his library—I knew the bookcases would be scattered throughout all those rooms. The colors would have to go, as he preferred the dark burgundies and forest greens. We held hands as we left the rooms—looked at each other—and KNEW this would be our home. At the door Marie whispered, "You are collectors and the house wants you."

The plans for our house were put into motion and we only awaited a signing date. However, I still lived in Edgewater with the kitty-cats. One evening my son, Wayne, called and needed to talk. I prepared dinner and over the food we discussed the events in our lives. It seemed he had just broken with his fiance. Her problem had worsened and he couldn't live with it. "I've just wasted a year of my life on this relationship," he bemoaned.

"Maybe you shouldn't look at it like that," I said. "Didn't you learn anything from the relationship?"

"Yeah, I guess I did. Especially, that I had better learn to control <u>my own</u> drinking—too much beer." And I guess I learned how to somewhat do a better job of controlling my temper."

"Then it wasn't a total waste…. you might even say the relationship was meant to be!"

He laughed, "O.K. Mom." After dinner we watched TV, but I could see he was restless. "Guess I'll go over and see Maggie—take her out for coffee—I could use a few laughs. We get along—yeah we get along." And that was how the "Maggie and Wayne" thing began.

◆   ◆   ◆

Don called to let me know the house signing was slated for August. Much sooner than I had expected. I did not want to live in the house as anything but Don's wife, and I wanted the Zanghi name, when I signed for our house. And so we talked. As much as I wanted our wedding date to be January the 28th, my spiritual rebirth, the day of the past-life regression, I had to save that as my spiritual rebirth anniversary not my wedding date. We looked at Don's calendar and he had free time in mid August. We decided on August 17th. Our wedding date; I was thrilled. I would be Mrs. Donald Zanghi on August 17th.

"1 don't want a big wedding," I told him. He was in complete accord, as we had both been through the big church wedding bit.

"Let's make it just you and me and the attendants—our own special day," he said hugging me. We thought of having the ceremony by Spirit Pond—but the weather was pretty humid. Then our friend the Rev. Richard Bengston (who would perform the ceremony) suggested Colby Temple. We agreed.

But I have discovered that the most simple plan can become suddenly elaborate when dealing with the <u>Donald</u>. "We have to have a 'special' ceremony," he pondered.

"Special—like what?" I inquired.

"I don't know yet—but spirit will give the theme."

"UMM," I thought.

Then there was the matter of the wedding bands. Mine, was simple—I just wanted a narrow gold ring. But Don wanted something unique. "What are you looking for?" I inquired as we trudged from jewelry store to jewelry store, to pawn shops, to gift shops, to flee markets. "I don't know, but it will be a special band because I'm marrying you." And so the week—long search continued. Until we finally found the wide silver band completely encircled with ankhs—the Egyptian cross symbolizing eternity. Later, he said, "What do you think of an Egyptian theme for our wedding?"

The very first past life I had seen with Don was Egyptian. What did I think—I couldn't be happier.

That evening Maggie came visiting. There was something unusual about her. She looked at me and there were stars in her eyes. The woman actually glowed. "Maggie, something wonderful has happened to you. What—tell me—tell me!"

"It's Wayne." Her voice was soft and dulcet. "We have been seeing each other every night. It is happening so fast. He even mentioned our buying a house together." Maggie, my best friend in Edgewater, and my son. It was perfect—she was perfect for him. I couldn't have dreamed up a better combination.

I hugged her and expressed my joy. "Mag, it couldn't be better. I know you two will wind up together. It's just perfect, Mag."

"And it all began with the journey to Cassadaga. I knew you, and then met your son, and you met Don. It all began with <u>the journey to Cassadaga</u>," she concluded.

"What a difference a year makes. You were lonely, you lost Buffie kitty, you were working—just existing. I was taking Mom to the Pentecostal church, and spending time with a lover. Now you will be with Wayne, and I will live in a spiritualist community with Don. What a difference a year makes! And think how Spirit can come in like a tornado and change our lives. We should never give up on life—we should always realize Spirit has surprises for us." I exclaimed.

Spirit had had another surprise for me. I was writing this book, even though the wedding plans were being formulated. One day I learned, through spirit, that my writing guide had brought in a writer from the spirit world to aid me—no else a personage than—Elizabeth Barrett Browning. I was blown away that so great a spirit personage would come to me in my hours of work. I was humbled and amazed.

In one of our lyceums the Rev. Linda Wade told us Spiritualism is getting out there into the real world. She told us the police department had requested help, not in solving a crime, but in counseling the mother of a murder victim. The mother was acting suicidal, and Linda was asked to give counsel to this distraught woman. This re-emphasizes that we are a Spiritualist community—we are a community of brotherhood—a community that believes in Infinite Intelligence and the Golden Rule.

August 17th was getting closer and closer. We planned to go to the Carolinas' for our honeymoom. I couldn't wait to go with Don! How wonderful to be alone with him for a whole week. This would be unusual as he is a people person, and people are drawn to him. Having him to myself for a week would be a unique treat. Even if it took a honeymoon to do it!

Then there was the matter of our attendants. No problem with Don. He chose his very close friend and TM teacher, Laurence Topliffe. But I had the problem. I, naturally, thought of my sister, Doris. But that posed the problem, if we wanted a small wedding. If my sister was the matron of honor—then my sons and whole family must be invited, and if my whole family attended—Don's whole family had to be considered. And that meant a big wedding. So, the problem was solved by asking Maggie to be my attendant…

The big day was mere days away. I looked around the Edgewater home and realized I was leaving a small bit of my heart here: I thought of all the dinners, all the friends and relatives that visited, and Peter. Peter my lover had been a part of my life for over fifteen years, and now he must remain here…. a part of my past. But, my kitty-cats (Don tolerated them), would go with me. "You, my monsters, are part of my past and my present," I told them. I would remain in the apartment until the kitchen of the Cassadaga house was remodeled. The owners had told Don he could begin moving his things from his apartment to a couple of rear rooms. Then there was the matter of notifying the upstairs tenant so he could move his metaphysical artifacts there. I would move in after I had rented the Edgewater town-house. It would probably be a couple of months before I could actually reside in our home. But I knew we would keep the road hot between Cassadaga and Edgewater: a whirl of plans and I was ready for them.

I had introduced Don to the family as a lecturer and counselor. My daughter-in-law kept saying, "But exactly what do you lecture about?" I always found a truthful but evasive answer. They seemed to like Don and certainly found it preferable to my relationship with Peter.

"As soon as I feel they really, really like you I'll tell them about Cassadaga and Spiritualism," I told Don. "I think in some cases it will make a difference." True, sad, but true. My sister, of course, believes like I do and had been in on the fact right along. Mom, cried about it, thinking Spiritualism was not true Christianity and my soul must surely be in jeopardy. She still liked Don, but gave him a bad time about Spiritualism on many occasion. My two oldest sons accepted it as part of my new life. They would accept Don and I knew I could invite them to Cassadaga and my home there. However, my youngest son (a fundamentalist Christian) told me he could not visit Cassadaga as it was on satanic grounds. He continued to treat Don with friendliness, unlike his wife who displayed a coldness toward him. She, also, felt Cassadaga housed evil. This attitude hurt, but I knew it was <u>their</u> problem and perhaps in time they would see Don and Spiritualism in the light of truth. Other friends and relatives simply accepted it as part of my new life and were happy for me.

And now we were planning the last—minute details of our wedding. Don would prepare a table with Egyptian artifacts in front of the altar at Colby Temple. What to wear—for this Egyptian theme without looking in "costume"? Don chose a black shirt with banded collar—he would wear his multitude of ankh jewelry and complete the look with black trousers and a colorful Egyptian print vest. I had a couple of outfits in mind—one of white lace—and the other a black lace skirt; topped with a black vest encrusted with pearls. Don said, "I like them both-surprise me." And so we both wound up in black splashed with color. I needed something for my headdress. I rummaged through my hats and found an antique evening hat which was perfect: It was simply rounded velvet tubes encircling the top of the head and voila one tube, directly in the front, went upward over the forehead to form a rhinestone encrusted "Snake." Could it be more perfect—Cleopatra's asp? Don had his Egyptian bride—for the second time.

August 17th dawned: a beautiful Southern day. The phone jangled and I reached from under the covers for the call. "How's my bride-to-be?" Don inquired.

"No, cold feet?" I inquired.

"How could I have cold feet when we have done this in so many lifetimes?" He laughed. "And didn't you say you had retrieved from memory two <u>more</u> lifetimes!" And yes, I had seen the vision of us in India plodding along behind an ox, and in the orient where we were dressed in colorful fabric and surrounded by influential people. Only God knows how many more lifetimes there were to recall.

I knew Don would call again during the day. He and his friends would take the heavy oak round table from his apartment to Colby Temple where Don would make it into an Egyptian fantasy. I would as I promised, pick up a bouquet of flowers for the table, and I would carry white flowers.

Getting dressed that evening, I was nervous. My kitty-cats knew, as they mewed and rubbed around my ankles. I put on a more glamorous cosmetic, my outfit and finally, the crowning touch—the Egyptian—asp hat. I smiled back at myself from the mirror. Maggie was outside waiting when I walked the few steps to her apartment. She looked lovely in a simple, long, navy dress. "Jeanette," she exclaimed, "you look gorgeous." She was not the type to lavish compliments, so I was impressed.

She started the car and I said, "Another journey, Mag," "we started out last August together on the first journey to Cassadaga, and here we are together a year later on the final journey. We have completed the circle."

We were strangely quiet on the journey. I seemed to be wrapped in an eternal haze—the whole evening seemed like everything was wrapped in a special hazy significance. I felt radiant: I felt like a bride. Not just any bride—I had been a bride before in this lifetime. No, I was marrying my soulmate. The heavens smiled and I was wrapped in special glory.

Suddenly, we were at Don's apartment. He rushed over to kiss me, and said, "I knew you would wear the dark outfit: you look beautiful."

"No fair having psychic powers," I laughed, "I can't really ever surprise you!"

Laurence arrived. "Look at my handsome husband," I exclaimed. I had never thought Don looked the Sicilian Italian—but more like a mysterious sheik or someone very exotic and foreign. We four walked the few steps to Colby Temple. There wasn't another person on the street, and even the houses appeared empty. It was like the four of us, walking down that street, were the only people in the world—and we walked in that special glow—that special ethereal haze.

We entered the enormous maw of the temple. I looked past the rows of chairs to the lectern and gasped. Front and center was Don's masterpiece—the Egyptian table. "Oh, Don," I said, with tears in my eyes, "It is truly a fantasy." I rushed forward to get a better look. He had covered the table in fringed gold patterned brocade. He had hung the blue and gold pharaoh picture on the alter rail, a pharaoh bust rested beneath the picture. Plumes of russet stood in tall vases flanking the table. Candles, chakra candles, glowed in a colorful arc on the rear of the table. Two sphinx resided on each side, lighted by blue candles in golden holders. A green pyramid was centered between the sphinx. Our favorite Egyptian cups were front and center. And then, the bouquet of flowers was centered on the floor in front of the table. It was Don's creation and our wedding masterpiece.

Barbara Joy Bengston joined us with camera in hand. We would have pictured memories. Don and I held hands, listening to Richard's instructions for the ceremony. This was happening, this was really happening. The circle was being completed-I would be reunited with Don again—here in Colby Temple.

As from a distance I heard Richard begin the ceremony "Beloved friends we have come here in the presence of God and these witnesses to unite this man and woman in the bonds of holy matrimony. Marriage is an honorable state and the institution of the homes: one of the important bases of civilization.

"Our friends have made their choice of life partners, and now stand before us that we may witness the holy covenant."

"Therefore if any can show just cause why they should not be joined together let him speak now, or here after hold his peace."

Don squeezed my hand and my love was suddenly tearing down my face as Richard spoke of marital love and responsibilities.

"The golden rule in married life is mutual Forbearance…. We urge each not to be the first by whom the harsh word is spoken, nor the last to offer the hand of reconciliation.

"It is fervently to be hoped that you will prove to each other suitable companions through life, and be knit together, not only with the silken cords of affection, but with a bond that strengthens with years and brightens with age, the bond of congenial tastes, intellectual and spiritual attachments one for the other."

I looked at Don and we smiled. There were tears in those eyes of love. I have never seen anyone look at me like that—complete and unconditional love. My heart was near to bursting with joy.

Richard instructed, "Jeanette, conserve and cherish the sacredness of home. Make it the altar at which you worship, and be sure that domestic bliss is within the reach of all who intelligently strive to attain it.

"Don, now that you have won a loving heart guard it with zealous care, nor ever let the storms of anger arise to wither true affection with its fiery breath. Never forget that love, unaccompanied by true companionship, soon droops under the chilling influence of uncongeniality of mind.

"To both of you: So live that when the evening of life arrives you may exclaim with the poet, 'Not another joy like this in all the world.'"

We were wrapped in that ethereal glow—we were wrapped in that special joy.

Don took my right hand and looked into my eyes saying, "I, Donald James Zanghi take thee Jeanette Mary Strack to be my lawful wedded wife, for better, for worse, for richer, for poorer, in sickness and in health, to love honor and cherish from this day forth."

And I took his right hand and hoped I could get through the words audibly, "I, Jeanette Mary Strack, take thee Donald James Zanghi to be my lawful wedded husband, for better, for worse, for richer, for poorer, in sickness and in health; to love, honor and cherish from this day forth."

Richard asked for the ring and said, "The ring is the symbol of conjugal union, it is endless as eternity. May the circle ever remind you of your sacred union from this day forward." And then he prayed "Eternal Spirit, we pray that this ring shall bless the wearer and honor the giver, that these two who shall become one, in flesh and in spirit, shall live together in perfect peace. Amen."

Richard gave Don the ring and Don put the ring on my finger, but got a look of panic in his eyes—the ring went as far as the knuckle. I smiled and gave it the extra push it needed to slip into place. And Don said, "Jeanette, with this ring I thee wed."

Richard gave me Don's ring—I had no problem slipping it on his finger. "Don, with this ring I thee wed."

"For as much as Don and Jeanette have pledged their mutual vows, and have given and received a ring in token of the same, I by the authority vested in me as a Minister of Spiritualism in accordance with the laws of this State, do pronounce you Husband and Wife."

The benediction was said, "May the blessings of Eternal Spirit be with you. May the angels of the greater life ever be near you. May peace be your portion, and happiness your constant companion from this day forth. Amen." And the bride was thoroughly kissed. Congratulations rang. We went out into the evening wrapped in our special glow. Don opened the car door and said, "Your chariot, Mrs. Zanghi." My new name spoken by my husband. We would all go to a very special restaurant in the Florida pines, and then to our Edgewater house, and then off to the Carolina Mountains for our honeymoon.

Twilight was descending as we drove through the peaceful streets of Cassadaga. I felt the presence of Elizabeth Barrett Browning. I looked at Don and smiled: I could hear echoes of past—life weddings: the solemnity of our Egyptian wedding, the chants of the Indian ceremony, and the pomp and splendor of our English wedding. But, in this lifetime, after years of searching—we had found each other. Could anything equal our union at Colby Temple? I felt that our car was a chariot pulled by white horses riding into the sunset, and that we would live

Happily

Ever

After.

◆   ◆   ◆

What has this journey meant to me? I am filled with more abundant life. God allowed me to meet my soul mate on this plane. I am filled with joy as I study and go forward in my soul's progression. I go forward peeling off layer after layer, reaching deeper and deeper into God-realization.

What will this book mean to Don? I hope the book will mean Don will reach more and more people as a healer and as a medium. It will inspire him to write HIS book on case histories and past-life regressions. He is truly one of those God-like men.

And what can this book mean to the reader? Perhaps your path in the search for God has not fully satisfied your soul. Cast off your burdens, take up your quest, and join Don and me on the JOURNEY TO CASSADAGA.

END

0-595-22013-4